Return
to
Responsibility

Constraints on
Autonomy
in Higher Education

Paul L. Dressel and William H. Faricy

with the assistance of
Philip M. Marcus and F. Craig Johnson

Foreword by Frederick de W. Bolman

RETURN
TO
RESPONSIBILITY

 Jossey-Bass Inc., Publishers
San Francisco • Washington • London • 1972

RETURN TO RESPONSIBILITY
Constraints on Autonomy in Higher Education
By Paul L. Dressel and William H. Faricy
with the assistance of Philip M. Marcus and F. Craig Johnson

Copyright © 1972 by Jossey-Bass, Inc., Publishers

Published in Great Britain by
Jossey-Bass, Inc., Publishers
St. George's House
44 Hatton Garden, London E.C.1

Library of Congress Catalogue Card Number LC 70-186574

International Standard Book Number ISBN 0-87589-136-5

Manufactured in the United States of America

JACKET DESIGN BY WILLI BAUM

FIRST EDITION

Code 7220

The Jossey-Bass
Series in Higher Education

sions? The answer is simple—and to many if not to most people totally unacceptable: politicians, quasi-political groups, professionals, and students. And no group will yield power or influence. Sudden unselfish intelligence is not likely to dawn equally among these groups to bring harmony and coordination of effort. The resulting issues and conflicts and unused opportunities must be viewed as part of any highly organized effort in our society—government, business, or the professions, for example.

Basic in these circumstances is to diagnose the ever changing kind, quality, and pragmatic purpose of autonomy, accountability, and constraint in the university—all universities in their several ways. The nicety of Dressel's diagnosis is that he shows there is nowhere a single answer and never a permanent cure. Even if man—through his organized efforts—should succeed in achieving goals, he would still have to tolerate huge amounts of ambiguity and change. Fire, the wheel, and $e = mc^2$ were once solutions in a sense; but then they created new uncertainties and new change.

Any politician, businessman, educator, or student who reads this book is likely at some point to be angered at what the authors say. The reader is well advised at that point to question whether the view he holds is not simply a nostrum and as such untherapeutic. It is not that the authors claim superior insight or assume that their conclusions alone are right and good. However, they have gathered impressive empirical evidence both in the United States and in England for the need to change our habits of thought and action. I know of no clearer statement, presented in great detail, of the immense need to plan on a state, regional, and finally national basis for the allocation and management of our higher education resources.

New York
February 1972

FREDERICK DEW. BOLMAN
Executive Director
Esso Education Foundation

Preface

In many respects this volume is a sequel to the study of university departments reported in *The Confidence Crisis*. Here we consider at length some of the issues raised in that book. In the earlier study, we found that administrators and departments had contrasting views about priorities and that both sides were dissatisfied with internal and external relationships and with involvement in decision making. We found that the "best" departments in the "better" universities tended to place research and graduate instruction at the apex of the priorities. We also found that departments were inclined to justify their requests for resources on whatever grounds they thought would be successful and to utilize their resources in accordance with their own priorities. Departmental and professional autonomy thus has led to irresponsibility. Since universities have refused to account for their stewardship, accountability is being thrust upon them.

This second phase of our study focuses on developments, self-generated or externally imposed, designed to bring increased control over the use of resources in the university. The appropriate degree of autonomy of the university and its units is a central issue which inevitably becomes a theme running through all the discussion. We are not looking for organizations, management and data, or budgeting systems solely to get departments under control. Rather we are looking for patterns of reorganization and patterns of resource development and allocation based upon definite plans and roles for individual institutions and the units in them. We seek also for procedures that will provide for accountability in the use of resources.

To these ends, we look at the impact of state coordination on institutions and departments. We look at reorganizations within institutions: undergraduate residential colleges, new groupings of departments, distinctions between graduate and undergraduate faculty. We also look at the use of management information systems that attempt to account for all functions and all funds in the context of institutional roles. We are also interested in plans and procedures that present new approaches to allocation of resources. We are aware of certain difficulties with the departmental pattern, and we are looking at new developments to ask whether these result in a university more flexible in its planning, more knowledgeable about the way its resources are utilized, and more effective in the performance of the several functions.

This volume is largely about the problem of balancing the forces of centralization and decentralization. We seek to ease that problem by considering various new organizations and reorganizations and by suggesting some policies which may be determined centrally but administered with some freedom by each institution.

The organization of this volume arises directly out of the preceding considerations. After a review in Chapter One of the present crises in the university and the inner and external threats to its autonomy, Chapter Two considers autonomy and academic freedom. Chapter Three reports a survey of opinions related to the roles of various persons and groups in decision making or review of decisions. Chapter Four looks at new organizational structures, particularly at their significance for undergraduate education. Chapters Five through Eight consider various developments in coordination, budgeting, planning, and faculty involvement in decision making. Chapter Nine summarizes our emerging views about the impact of organizational developments and innovations in correcting the deficiencies of universities and states our convictions about the constraints that must be imposed upon universities if they are to function in a responsive and responsible way to meet the needs of society.

The volume focuses primarily on the large public university, but the trend toward public support of private universities and the necessity of including private institutions in the planning of higher education convince us that most of what we have to say has relevance now and will have more in the future for all of higher education. We reinforce this conviction by occasional brief interpolations at strategic points, but we are content to leave to the reader and to the future the ultimate resolution of the task of coordinating private and public higher education.

Many of the views and recommendations presented may not be widely acceptable. We wish, indeed, that we could have concluded that the universities are able to govern themselves responsibly. We are not pleased with what emerges. There was much to be said for the autonomous, opportunistic approach; it made for an exciting life (as the senior author, after well over thirty years at Michigan State University, is well aware). But higher education has become a big business, the earlier model is no longer reasonable, and only external restraints will control the aspirations of the many institutions that still wish to emullate Harvard, Michigan, and California.

We express thanks to the administrators and faculty of the institutions visited; all of them cooperated fully with us in interviews. We also thank the many faculty members, administrators, board members, and legislators who responded to our questionnaire and, in many cases, wrote at some length about the issues. Special thanks are due Frederick deW. Bolman, executive director of the Esso Education Foundation, for his assistance in acquiring the grant that supported this project and for his warm personal interest in it. Ruth Frye, who has suffered through and contributed to most of our studies and publications, contributed very significantly to this one. Marion Jennette and Sheila Hoeve were of major assistance in many ways.

East Lansing, Michigan
February 1972

PAUL L. DRESSEL
WILLIAM H. FARICY

Contents

Return
to
Responsibility

Constraints on
Autonomy
in Higher Education

I

Universities in Crisis: Threats to Autonomy

Despite occasional setbacks, universities during the past twenty years have experienced unprecedented growth in students, facilities, faculty, programs, and dollars. In a number of institutions, increases in funds resulting from increased student enrollments were diverted to new and costly programs of uncertain merit and unverified need. In following years, these programs were used to "justify" demands for even more resources, and rivalry among institutions in pursuit of national or international prominence inflated the demands. Autonomy fathered irresponsibility. By the late 1960s, this situation became evident to those outside the universities who provided the support and even to many persons within universities whose taxes and children's education costs also continued to rise.

Today universities are finding that autonomy is never absolute and that their irresponsibility may destroy their au-

tonomy and make them obsolete. Philosophers and social
scientists always knew this, but they were ignored as long as
the universities were able to enjoy the rewards of autonomy.
Autonomy, fed by federal grants and contracts as well as state
funds, became virtually synonymous with academic freedom
and with professional competency. Since professional competency clearly rests in the faculty, the role of administrations,
boards, legislators (in the faculty conception) was not to reason
why but simply find the cash. Faculties demanded the right to
do what they considered interesting or important even if that
did not, as in fact it turned out, include undergraduate education.

The university's purposes—instruction, research, and
service—do not exist as isolated, unrelated factors; for the
university as a whole performs a service to society. It meets
some of the immediate needs of society for trained personnel,
increased knowledge, and so on, and also provides leadership
for seeking a better society. Instruction and research are elements of this service and thus cannot be based solely on the
preferences and judgment of the faculty. However, both the
faculty and the administration tend to assume that, although
society is obliged to support the institution, the superior intel-
lect and judgment within the institution justify its moving in
whatever directions it (the administration and faculty) feels
desirable. The university (like the department) in seeking support from the public makes its case on one set of considerations
but, having obtained the resources, uses them to increase the
stature of the university by permitting faculty members to
impose their own priorities. This is inconsistent with the view
that the university (whether public or private) exists to carry
out certain purposes delegated by society and must fulfill these
purposes as effectively and economically as possible.

A university behaving responsibly in its search for resources would indicate exactly how the resources are to be used.
It would recognize that those who supply the resources may
have ideas about the value of various programs and may allocate resources accordingly. The university would also render
an accounting of how resources were actually used and what

was accomplished thereby. Obviously, there are difficulties with this conception of responsibility. There is some point to the argument that many members of the legislatures do not really understand the nature of higher education and that therefore full revelation of university operations is unwise. But even though irresponsibility and dishonesty are sometimes displayed in political processes, such failings hardly provide justification for university intellectuals to set themselves above the democratic process and demand complete autonomy. If we believe in higher education as a value-oriented enterprise responsible to the society that supports it, then the university should approach its various publics with forthrightness rather than concealment and provide a paradigm of the behavior upon which a democratic society is predicated.

Autonomy must be earned and continuously justified; otherwise, the insistence on autonomy creates mistrust, reprisal, and demands for accountability. The survival of the university itself is at stake. Today, some members of universities seek a radical solution and would welcome the university's demise, assuming that, phoenix-like, it would be reborn with a new sense of responsibility and responsiveness to society. But certainly mere survival is no more the goal of the university than is uncontrolled growth.

Growth, which has been at the root of many university problems, continues to be viewed as a goal by many administrators (Hodgkinson, 1970b). In their quest for greatness (synonymous, in their view, with growth) these administrators bargained away their own authority by encouraging and responding to faculty demands. Thereby was created an uneasy and unholy alliance in which administrators became instruments of faculty aspirations and together they basked in each other's approval. When resources became short and cutbacks were required, administrators did not find the same cooperation. Recently, one university faced simultaneously a reduced legislative appropriation and a faculty demand for a 14 per cent salary increase, supported by threats of faculty unionization. Administrators were expected to find the dollars without faculty cooperation in determining where internal cutbacks might be made and with overt resistance to any review of faculty load or departmental budgets. Preoccupation with institutional growth gave low priority to educating students. But student disruptors, supported by segments of the faculty, brought the growth of universities to a halt.

Addition of the student voice brings further dilution of power and authority, increases the time spent in deliberation, broadens the range of concerns, introduces new values, and multiplies the number of conflicts to be resolved. And so in the university today no one can say who decides what, and no one even knows who gets to decide who decides what. Moreover, faculties, insistent on their prerogatives in policy making, have generally demonstrated their inability to agree on action. They waste endless hours writing high-sounding, ambiguous, and unenforceable policies. The situation is ripe for external intervention (Altbach, 1960).

External intervention may even be necessary to preserve campus freedoms. The intellectual autonomy of the campus, as well as academic freedom, has been diminished in recent years by a few willful faculty, students, and nonstudents, who refused a hearing to contradictory views or informed analyses by speakers whose past statements or involvements have incurred the displeasure of extremists (left or right). Intervention by administrators or by external agencies has been seized by such bigots as a means of dramatizing their cause, rallying support for it, and justifying their *a priori* characterizations of those who intervene. And so the extremists took a calculated series of steps, each step more inflammatory than the preceding, until the intervention was countered with allegations of violation of constitutional rights. In the public confrontation or legal recourse that followed, the original actions were forgotten or deemed irrelevant.

Constraints on free speech and open discourse constitute a deeply serious threat to the university if one accepts our view that mere survival is not the goal. And these constraints are precursors of others. The aura of scholarly detachment and objectivity surrounding the university has been in danger of being dissipated by the disorderly and destructive behavior of faculty and students. The identification of the university faculty and administrators with partisan resolution of sensitive social issues also endangers academic freedom. Doffing the academic habit, the professor becomes merely another human being; and when the professor fiddles beyond his expertise, the public burns.

The concept of tenure is currently under attack. Scully (1971) reports that at least five state legislatures have introduced bills to limit or to reexamine tenure at state institutions. Students and administrators are raising questions about tenure because it appears to protect faculty members who want to avoid undergraduates. Challenges to tenure also arise from legislators, who repeatedly are told that program cutbacks and budget reductions are impossible because of the presence of tenured faculty.

> The American Council on Education's Special Committee on Campus Tensions . . . called for a reexamination of tenure, noting that it has "sometimes been a shield for indifference and neglect of scholarly duties."
>
> The President's Commission on Campus Unrest . . . commented: "As one means of improving the quality of teaching in higher education, we urge reconsideration of the practice of tenure."
>
> The recently released report of a federally initiated task force on higher education called for "a revision of standard tenure policies leading toward short-term contracts for at least some categories of faculty positions."
>
> Critics of tenure argue that it is no longer needed as a guarantor of academic freedom, and that the economic security it gives to professors hurts a college's efforts to fulfill its "obligation to students and society."
>
> Many expect that the concept of academic freedom will be defined far more narrowly than the AAUP would like—to include only the actions of a faculty member in his classroom and in his scholarship [Scully, 1971, p. 4].

COURTS STRESS DUE PROCESS

But while institutions and the legislatures move in one direction, courts move in the opposite. This recent trend for

courts to limit university operations is typified by this report in
The Chronicle of Higher Education, May 3, 1971:

> A federal court . . . enjoined Youngstown State Uni-
> versity from dismissing a nontenured assistant professor "un-
> less and until he has been given both a written statement of
> the reasons for his dismissal and an opportunity for a hearing
> at which to contest such a decision." . . . The university [in-
> dicated that it does] not plan to appeal the decision . . . [and
> noted that] a regulation prohibits stating reasons for not re-
> newing contracts with nontenured faculty members.
>
> Judge Frank J. Battista said: "On the evidence before
> it, the court finds that the defendant university's termination
> of plaintiff's employment, by failing to renew his contract of
> employment without disclosing the reasons for such termina-
> tion, constitutes arbitrary and capricious conduct prohibited
> by the due process clause of the Fourteenth Amendment, and
> violates plaintiff's rights under the federal civil rights statutes."

This decision is similar to a 1970 decision in a federal
court in Wisconsin: the judge ordered Wisconsin State University at Oshkosh either to grant a hearing to an assistant
professor whose contract had not been renewed or to reappoint
him. An appeal is now pending before the U.S. Supreme Court.

INCURSIONS FROM LEGISLATURES

Crowl (1971) reports on various forms of legislation that
would restrict state colleges and universities in a number of
states. Proposals in Iowa would end tenure and sabbatical leaves
for faculty members and would set enrollment limits at state
universities. Bills in Florida and New York set a minimum
number of hours that faculty members must spend in classroom teaching. (The Florida bill is now a law; the New York
bill was passed, but the legislature recalled it for further study.)
A New York law suspends sabbatical leaves for all state employees for one year, including faculty at state colleges and
universities. A rider to an appropriations bill in Minnesota
would channel all university funds through the state treasurer.
The University of Minnesota, which claims that the rider vio-

lates its constitutional autonomy, may seek a court test if it is enacted. Obviously legislatures are seeking various ways to keep a closer eye on university affairs.

A second controversial law passed by the 1971 New York legislature expresses the "sense of the legislature" that educators should devote more time to classroom teaching. It specifies that community college teachers should have fifteen "classroom contact" hours per week and that teachers at four-year undergraduate colleges and graduate institutions should have twelve hours and nine hours, respectively. Similar laws have been enacted in other states. The final status of the measure is still in doubt, however. After passing the bill and sending it to Governor Nelson A. Rockefeller, the legislature recalled it for further consideration.

Tennessee has the following provisions:

Before making salary changes, the higher education administrators must consult with Tennessee Higher Education Commission and the state department of finance and administration. The commissioner of finance and administration, the state comptroller, and the commission will prescribe procedures for submitting work programs, operating budgets, plus any revisions.

In actual practice, this means colleges and universities must submit work programs, operating budgets, and proposed revisions to the higher education commission. THEC will have a chance to make comments before passing the proposals along to the finance and administration commissioner.

Final authority to approve or reject the changes and proposals rests with the commissioner. In the past, however, revisions have been routinely approved; now they will be subject to closer scrutiny as a result of the THEC and its staff's being accorded an opportunity to file comments and recommendations.

University of Tennessee found itself confronted with one not wholly welcome development when the legislature directed the university's medical school to establish a department of family medicine and provided $150,000 to finance it. Though UT medical unit administrators were agreeable to new emphasis upon the general practice of medicine, they resented the legislature ordering a department established for that purpose [Southern Regional Education Board, 1971].

These examples of intervention underline the fact that university autonomy is being weakened. One may readily infer from the nature of the incursions that legislatures and courts doubt the ability of the university to govern itself.

Moos and Rourke (1959, pp. 283–284) pointed out a major cause for this situation:

> One of the common reasons for legislative intrusion on educational administration has been the lack . . . of full information from universities regarding campus operations and plans. Some of the mightiest state universities in the country have suffered severe appropriation cuts in recent sessions, partly if not entirely because of their unwillingness to make a complete disclosure of information requested by the legislature. Although college officials may have had good reason for their reluctance to impart certain information to the legislature, their explanations did nothing to change the shrinking appropriations.
>
> Some universities have balked at disclosing their method of computing student enrollment, leaving themselves wide open to the charge that they are padding enrollment figures in order to get higher appropriations. This reluctance has given impetus to the movement to establish state-wide formulas for computing enrollments. Other schools have refused to disclose information on costs at the same time as they have asked for large increases in appropriations. The legislative reaction is to assume that chaos governs fiscal policies on the campus.

British universities apparently have also overlooked their social and financial responsibilities. In early 1971 the London *Daily Telegraph* carried articles characterizing the Ph.D.s produced by the universities as "so narrowly specialized and blinkered" that industry finds them useless (January 14, 1971). Suggestions by industrialists that universities should include more applied courses apparently have not changed academic attitudes and practices, but the lack of jobs for the theoretically oriented disciplinary specialist may produce change simply because students will not continue for long to seek an unmarketable degree. In an article on January 20, 1971, the *Daily Telegraph* reports that financial problems have caused reduction in sabbatical leaves at Cambridge and that prospective deficits in other universities have caused them to forgo purchasing books and equipment and the hiring of additional staff. Meanwhile, the British universities complain about the lack of support for graduate students and, much like American universities, insist on producing degrees no one wants while deficits threaten.

Cheit (1971) reports that twenty-nine of forty-one colleges and universities in his study are in financial difficulty or headed for it. Universities headed for trouble may make program cuts and change plans, but primarily they postpone planned growth in existing programs or the addition of new ones. "To finance new programs, 'new' money is required, but there is no 'new' money. To go ahead with plans would mean transferring 'old' money away from an existing program commitment to a new one. . . . These are painful cuts, and to make them in the interests of new programs requires commitment to a plan, criteria for performance and output, and administrative authority beyond what is found on campuses headed for financial trouble, whether in this study or not" (Cheit, 1971, p. 85).

According to Cheit, universities in serious financial difficulty have looked more deeply into cutting costs by program elimination, and some have begun to drop departments and graduate majors. But most responses are still of the belt-tightening variety. Cheit notes that the typical response of all categories of schools is to seek more funds, especially from private sources. The tendency always seems to be to resort to trimming fringes, avoiding any real cuts or eliminations, hoping always that after a brief period, two or three years at most, the merry game of growth can be resumed at an accelerated rate. Here rivalry among institutions inhibits selective pruning. One provost confided that, if worse came to worst, he might discard a few programs but probably none of those duplicated elsewhere in the state. This university simply did not get the message. Perhaps few have.

Bailey (1969, p. 153) sums up the inadequate response that higher education has made to this many-sided, enervating crisis:

> By and large, higher education has been slow to innovate, slow to discard the obsolete. By and large, it is woefully sloppy on matters of rudimentary management. All too many faculties are "dog-in-the-mangerish" about academic housekeeping. The consequence is utilized and unutilized facilities that would have bankrupted profit-oriented institutions decades ago. Our personnel systems tend to be shoddy. We resist systematic evaluation by peers, students, alumni, or administrators and thereby are thrown into a jungle of unsystematic evaluations by the very same groups. The red herring of academic freedom is drawn across the path of systematic evaluation of performance. Basically the motivation is not defense of academic freedom at all, but fear of the insecure that their shortcomings might be verified or their sloth exposed.

Both government officials and the public are near a vote of no confidence in higher education. Universities are not obtaining the increased resources for which they clamor, are finding restraints imposed on their operations, are being told that there is no confidence in their requests for more money, and are being questioned about their ability to manage funds they already have. And, from what they have had, some will be taken away.

None of what has been said above is in any sense new. It simply presents the background for a developing feeling on our part that the department's ambitions, arrogance, and demands for independence are only indications that the department has observed, well understood, and faithfully followed the example set by the university. To change this pattern of irresponsibility, it seems to us that higher education must be regarded as a national resource, that the roles of institutions must be determined by social need, and that resources must be allocated according to a plan and their actual use accounted for. In moving in this direction, we are permitting the public and politicians to make decisions about the character of institutions, and their decisions may not always accord with the views of those involved in higher education. The task of the universities is to make their case forthrightly, back it up with all the evidence that they can bring together, and hope that support will be obtained. In so doing, universities cannot afford to be divided into competing groups demanding resources for one type of institution or for one institution over another. By this behavior, they force educational decisions to be made on political grounds.

Universities have lost the confidence of the public because they have ignored their social responsibilities and have demonstrated their inability to govern themselves effectively or to operate efficiently. A false sense of values has caused both faculty members and institutions to aspire to national recognition without consideration of the appropriate role of their institution or the desires of those who support it. The departmental disciplinary structure of the university is irrelevant to undergraduate education and increasingly irrelevant to the significant social issues. Organized by departments, budgeted by departments, and ultimately controlled by departments, the university has lost its ability to adjust to changing needs or to achieve a more economic operation based upon accepted purposes. Many universities, like their faculties, have become too engrossed in attaining national recognition and have lost their ability to examine critically programs and practices within the university and change them. Universities rarely display an ability to review their programs and eliminate duplicate or unsatisfactory ones. They refuse to cooperate with other universities in such ventures.

The ultimate solution for the problems of higher education will probably come from coordination and control, first at the state and then gradually at regional and national levels, extending to both public and private universities as the latter increasingly are supported from public funds. This development will undoubtedly raise serious questions about autonomy and academic freedom and lead to application of constraints on both. This book contains conclusions based on our belief that the imposition of role definitions and some operational controls on universities will not seriously interfere with their autonomy and that such controls have little to do with academic freedom.

2

Autonomy and
Academic Freedom

"The issue of university autonomy will never be finally solved. It can only be lived with," John Gardner has remarked (Berdahl, 1971, p. v). Complete autonomy would require complete financial independence, an unattainable state. Even those universities that have approached financial independence usually have been unable to curb their aspirations and maintain programs within assured income. University autonomy will not be achieved through financial independence. Neither can autonomy in the university involve complete isolation from society or from politics. Both public and private universities must continually interact with donors and public officials, whose attitudes may have significant implications for university support and aspirations. Autonomy ultimately depends upon a social assumption that the university's role is to search for truth and that it can effectively perform broader services to society only if it possesses some degree of autonomy. Autonomy inevitably involves responsibility, continual negotiation, and firm confidence between the university and those who support and benefit from it. The continuing need to interpret and fight for autonomy is the greatest security against its abuse.

University autonomy is essentially the freedom to use resources and to define and execute programs consonant with institutional purposes. Autonomy allows institutional differentiation and diversity. It permits the development of individual initiative and creativity. Especially it recognizes professional competency and its role in fulfilling the purposes of the university. Without any autonomy, the university probably could not exist as we understand the term. The university could not perform the essential functions that led to its creation.

Few critics of the university wish to destroy it completely. They generally concede that the university performs certain essential functions—transmission of the culture, creation of new knowledge, and training individuals for intellectual pursuits—and that these functions require a high degree of autonomy. But, in addition, universities provide knowledge and service to almost every group that requests it and encourage all who are capable to take more education. It is these latter functions that have caused vital public concern and subjected university autonomy to pressures and restraints. Problems of autonomy have arisen partly because universities and their faculties have assumed that unplanned growth and competition with other universities will produce better quality, diversity, and satisfaction of social needs than will development by plan.

Autonomy is easy enough to define in the abstract, but it is difficult to deal with in the concrete since its nature and extent vary in different situations. For example, a university may have great autonomy which it does not extend to its colleges, departments, and other operating units. In fact, some institutions have been dominated by a genial, avuncular, or paternalistic president who retains complete authority. If an institution with such a leader grows rapidly in both size and prestige, provides tangible benefits to the faculty, and generates a sense of progress, then the faculty may not be concerned about authoritarian governance. Legislatures, boards, and some faculty and students often prefer such a pattern because it makes clear where the power is and where influence must be brought to bear.

Autonomy may be affected in many subtle ways. Size, student and faculty demands, external pressures, indifference to academic matters, a new administrator who cannot quickly assimilate all the facets of a complex university, and a generalized social approval of democracy in decision making—such factors result ultimately in some decentralization of power. Once authority is delegated to lower levels of the academic hierarchy, it may also be extended to the individual, as traditionally has been true with choice of research projects, and may also apply to teaching. Extension of autonomy to individuals introduces great variation in the faculty's perceptions of goals and priorities, permitting diversion of resources to support activities that may not coincide with university priorities and may be considered irresponsible by some. Accountability is hardly enforceable when marked differences in values and priorities exist and when expected outcomes are imprecisely stated. Under these conditions autonomy has been interpreted by some faculty members as essential to academic freedom if not identical with it—an unfortunate and erroneous interpretation, which constitutes a serious hazard to program review, innovation, and accountability. Autonomy and academic freedom are by no means synonymous. An institution may be autonomous but restrict academic freedom. On the other hand, an institution may limit autonomy of organization, programs offered, and allocation of resources, and still preserve academic freedom in the pursuit of truth.

Universities seek autonomy for many reasons: to gain freedom and flexibility in resource allocation, curriculum planning, faculty promotion, and selection of faculty and administrators; to determine instructional practices and admissions policies; and to make decisions about research and educational programs. When a university keeps in mind resource commitments and social obligations, its autonomy is hardly subject to debate. Misuse of autonomy to the detriment of responsiveness to social needs and economic realities generates intervention. Misused autonomy also tends to produce uniformity rather than differentiation and diversity.

Berdahl (1971) distinguishes between procedural autonomy and substantive autonomy. In his view, procedural autonomy may be curbed by state controls imposed in the interest of good management without threatening the substantive autonomy or academic freedom. Many persons who have looked at state controls (as we shall do shortly) have taken a much more serious view of their implications. Berdahl's argument is that essential fairness in interpreting and imposing controls is of more importance than whether a particular control is, in itself, right or wrong. By fairness (whatever that may mean, and certainly it will be controversial) the public interest and the substantive autonomy of the universities will be protected. Perhaps the real point (also expressed by Berdahl) is that, since interference is inevitable, it should at any rate be confined to proper topics and controls should be expressed in a fair and sensitive fashion.

CONCEPTIONS OF ACADEMIC FREEDOM

In 1902 Professor Frederich Paulsen of the University of Berlin formulated an early (perhaps the original) conception of academic freedom that had become accepted in his country during the preceding decades: "It is no longer, as formerly, the function of the university teacher to hand down a body of truth established by authorities, but to search after scientific knowledge by investigation, and to teach his hearers to do the same. . . . For the academic teacher and his hearers there can be no prescribed and no proscribed thoughts. There is only one rule for instruction: to justify the truth of one's teaching by reason of the facts" (Fuchs, 1964, p. 5). Paulsen also expressed the view that political partisanship on the part of a faculty member is a disqualification, not withstanding the fact that professors may be "men of noble discontent" who sow "the thoughts for future acts." From this and other aspects of Paulsen's discussion, Fuchs concludes that Paulsen's view of academic freedom was internal to institutions of higher education and not applicable to external activities of academic personnel.

The current conception of academic freedom in American universities has been extended to include the right of the faculty member to express his views about world affairs. The university also requires strong emphasis on the rights of individuals to operate freely within their fields. Individuals must be free not only from external forces—politicians, trustees, parents, donors, alumni, or other groups—but also from internal factions that would distort the process of rational debate and discussion.

Certainly academic freedom in research and publication and in the classroom is augmented by personal freedom from institutional censorship or discipline when the faculty member, *regardless of field of study, speaks or writes as a citizen.* But academic and personal freedom must not be confused. According to Robert MacIver, "Academic freedom is a right claimed by the accredited educator, as teacher and as investigator, to interpret his findings and to communicate his conclusions without being subjected to any interference, molestation, or penalization because these conclusions are unacceptable to some constituted authority within or beyond the institution" (Murphy, 1964, p. 21). This restricted conception approximates that of Paulsen.

ACADEMIC FREEDOM IN RESEARCH

In at least one area, however, even this definition of academic freedom is being questioned. The classified research problem has raised serious discussions often forced by student pressures, on a number of campuses. We appear to be reaching the point of view that the univerity must put limits on the individual professor's freedom to develop his own research program. Partly as a result of demands from the National Institutes of Health, universities already have procedures for reviewing research proposals involving the use of human beings as experimental subjects. Investigators in medical and biological sciences have, for a long time, accepted restraints on their freedom in order to protect the rights of their subjects. Thus, the

experimenters in these areas seem relatively undisturbed by
new regulations. On the other hand, psychologists and social
scientists have resisted these policies as an assault on academic
freedom, and in some cases have demanded that regulations
be so stated that the review of a project rests at the departmental or individual level.

Now that universities have demonstrated not only the
power but the right to interfere with the freedom of individual
professors in choice of research topics and methods, one can
see that the integrity of universities has been threatened by
past practices. Federally supported applied-research programs
have been defined if not corrupted by the standing program
commitments of the agencies responsible for the programs. Policy postures of these agencies have seldom been challenged
openly, although often commented upon in scathing terms in
private. But the university, while seeming to respond only in
terms of proposals developed by faculty members, ends up by
accepting projects which compromise its integrity. It has accepted projects against the better judgments of deans and review committees simply because faculty members proposed
them and the funds were available. One may blame the faculty
members for placing the pursuit of funds ahead of principle,
but whenever grants influence the direction of inquiry, and
particularly influence it in directions of dubious merit, both
institutional integrity and individual autonomy require protection from temptation.

LIMITS OF ACADEMIC FREEDOM

The major emphasis in this country has been upon the
encouragement and protection of the freedom of the individual
faculty member, but irresponsible use of academic freedom by
the individual can threaten the character and the autonomy
of the university. The problem of such irresponsibility is too
serious to leave to any one individual, board, or external agency.
Hence, academic freedom has always a procedural as well as a
substantive aspect. The achievement and maintenance of academic freedom depends upon the creation of a system which,
on one hand, gives a teacher some measure of employment

security and, on the other, provides for some review and possibility of disciplining the teacher who abuses academic freedom. One of the difficulties in maintaining academic freedom is that scholars are notably remiss in censuring their colleagues; they tend to thrust the responsibility onto administrators and then sometimes delight in putting administrators on the spot because they have taken action.

The academic community will have to recognize that academic freedom, like most other freedoms, has its limits. In the last analysis, agreement on what the limits are can only be reached by some sort of political process. As a contribution to that process, we might begin by drawing a sharp distinction between the right of the university to determine the broad general directions of its research program and the right to tell individual investigators at a particular point in time what they can and cannot do. . . .

It seems likely that there would be far less tolerance in the academic community for the administrative decisions which prevent a particular individual from doing a given bit of research, in a field otherwise acceptable to the university, purely on the grounds that it gives promise of producing knowledge that might later be used in antisocial ways. Although individual investigators have withdrawn from following up their own discoveries, for example in molecular genetics, on such putative moral grounds, it would be a reckless dean who would force them to do so [Morison, 1970, p. 634].

Largely ignored in discussions of academic freedom and individual and departmental autonomy is an ancient principle, conflict of interest. This principle demands that under certain conditions individuals should not make decisions that directly affect them. Conditions are not easily defined, and they differ from one field to another. Judges and other public officials, particularly at the federal level, are expected to divest themselves of any interests that conceivably could interfere with the decisions that they make. But faculty members and departments seldom realize that their decisions on curriculum requirements, section size, grading policy, use of resources are heavily based upon their own self-interests. When this issue has been raised, the faculty has tended to confuse personal and institutional interests. The faculty member regards himself as a professional who obviously will make decisions that will advance the profession and advance the university in the process, but faculty debates on such a simple matter as course distribution requirements show that the motivation is often more based on departmental and professorial concerns than on the good of the student.

Academic freedom (and its alter ego, conflict of interest) is perhaps no more problematic in the contemporary university than straitened finances or outmoded curriculum, but—like student unrest—it can create issues that are peculiarly irritating to average citizens, whose understanding of the university is limited at best. The Angela Davis case at the University of California, Los Angeles, whatever its essential merits, certainly polarized public opinion on academic freedom and probably hurt the institution, at least in the short run. Thus, demands for academic freedom can add to a backlash demand for restrictions on university autonomy.

RESTRICTIONS ON INSTITUTIONAL AUTONOMY

Demands to restrict autonomy are especially dangerous today because they come from so many sources, take so many different forms, and attack the university at so many vulnerable points. Although the university itself is far from blameless on all counts, the justifications for restriction of university autonomy are not always truthful. When truthful, they may still be self-delusive and, of course, they may not be logical or valid. Some of the reasons given include inefficient use of resources, poor performance, irrelevance of a program to current needs, role assignments within a system, elimination of inequities, needs of society, regional educational needs, and uniformity. These words all have an aura of respectability. Unfortunately, what appears to one person as an inequity or inefficiency may appear to the benefited party as an obvious and reasonable recognition of merit and quality.

Faced with possible restrictions which seem to exhibit

complete lack of understanding or sympathy with the complexities of higher education, university administrators, boards, and faculty have sometimes conspired to conceal information, occasionally to modify it, and generally to avoid introduction of any reporting system that might reveal the true situation. Thus, there emerges a second category of justifications for restricting the autonomy of universities and their component units. Deceit and dishonesty justify a demand for more responsible behavior in the service of society and for full accountability in the use of funds.

There are *internal* restrictions on autonomy as well as *external* ones, as becomes evident when one considers that autonomy pertains to several levels within a university as well as to state coordinating boards and to central administrations of multicampus systems. Many internal restrictions on the autonomy of faculty members, departments, and universities already exist. Although the university originally resisted and contested many of them, it now finds these restrictions essential to constrain its own components. Most university libraries, for instance, restrict access to stacks and assess fines for overdue books. Traditional professorial privileges of indefinite withdrawal have often been restricted because of extensive abuse. In addition, standards for sizes of offices and types of office equipment have been imposed to eliminate envy and competition and to achieve more efficient use of space and resources. Limitations on outside consultation by faculty (with or without pay) exist in most universities, although these limits are resented, sometimes ignored, and often indifferently enforced. Participation in partisan politics is commonly restricted, with leaves of absence required for candidates. Professors who assign their self-authored textual materials for their own courses have abused their prerogatives and caused student complaints, thereby encouraging restrictive policies. Access to campus facilities (meeting rooms, laboratories, computer, mail service, and parking) is restricted because both students and faculty have been found to make inappropriate use of them, causing damage, excessive custodial costs, or complaints. Rules regarding keys, building closing hours, long-distance calls, and removal of equipment for off-campus use are common.

CONFICT OF AUTONOMY: UNIVERSITY AND DEPARTMENT

Autonomy within a university is obviously affected by the interdependence of its components. Dynamic tension between the university and its components is more typical than some fixed permanent allocation of autonomy. The pattern of autonomy shifts as it is extended to those who demonstrate responsible and effective use of it and withdrawn from those who do not. Since a university rarely succeeds in attaining excellence in all areas, often conscious decisions must be made to allocate resources so as to promote excellence in certain fields while supporting others at a minimal level; obviously such decisions affect the autonomy of the university units.

Departmental autonomy is affected by the resources available as well as by restrictions imposed upon their use. When funds can be obtained for specific projects from foundations or from federal agencies, departmental autonomy is increased. Some departments have even been successful in soliciting unrestricted funds to be used as the department wishes. Departments which obtain such funds from nonuniversity sources usually expect to continue to get their share of the university budget and even to increase it as external program support is gradually shifted to university funds. Thus, the increasing of departmental autonomy by adding external resources may encumber university funds and, in turn, restrict the university's autonomy.

Placing each department on a line item salary budget and assigning funds by categories curtails the department's autonomy. Equipment budgets can be itemized and expenditures prohibited for any item other than those originally approved. Positions (and dollars) vacated by retirement or resignation may be withdrawn from the department for redistribution. The university thereby gains more control over the use of its resources (an increase in autonomy).

Departmental autonomy can also be restricted by demands of other departments and colleges, by interests and influence of various campus groups, and by university commitments and goals. A mathematics department which provided special courses for students in business and engineering gained resources by this service, but chafed at the routine aspect of the extra load and at the compromises on course content and perhaps grading necessary for nonmajor students. Departmental autonomy is limited when students complain about advising; when graduate assistants demand continuing appointments, equitable salaries, and defined loads; and when administrators refuse to approve departmental recommendations on appointments, promotions, and salary adjustments.

University autonomy is weakened by its inability either to alter the organizational structure or to rise above it in order to improve operations. Each element of a university—business office, student personnel, departments, colleges—will be provoked by any threat to eliminate it or to reduce its budget. For example, many student affairs offices are currently overstaffed but few have been seriously reduced. Colleges of agriculture or home economics may be obsolete on some land-grant university campuses, but only a very resolute president dares to challenge their place in the university. New interdisciplinary programs have perished on the rocks of departmental obstinacy, a fact that has led some new institutions to adopt a nondepartmental structure. Duplicate courses and small classes may go unquestioned because faculty members are often more troubled about a challenge to their professional prerogatives than about their efficiency in using resources.

EXTERNAL PRESSURES FOR RESTRICTING AUTONOMY

External restrictions are even more extensive than internal restrictions, although often less apparent to the individual professor or student. Regional and professional accrediting groups constrain universities and their departments in many ways, such as setting standards for program size, faculty qualifications, facilities, and equipment. Legislatures impose quotas on out-of-state students in most state universities. Many universities have been compelled, partly by demand of activist students and faculty, to impose limits on the research grants and contracts accepted. Federal agencies making grants for research require formulation and approval of policy statements. Codes of teaching responsibility, statements of due process, restrictions on access to information for students and faculty also exemplify the necessity of constraints to assure individual rights.

The chicanery in big-time varsity athletics—double standards in admissions, grants-in-aid, work programs, and hidden subsidies—probably results more from external than internal pressures. More than one university and legislature has been saddled with continuing support of a special-purpose building that is ill suited to present programs. Alumni of a particular college or program quickly rise to support it if program alterations or budget cuts threaten its existence. Local businessmen (realtors, bookstore owners, for example) watch the university closely and quickly protest, with threats of recourse to law, any practices which they see as unfair competition.

Legislatures, by their appropriation powers, present one of the most serious sources of interference; at various times and places they have tried to legislate the value of pi, eliminate a professor by deleting his salary, specify teaching loads, determine curriculum by requiring specific courses, force elimination of programs or addition of new ones by specific appropriations. The U.S. Office of Education is currently forcing universities to review their practices and policies in hiring women. Other less justifiable—some subtle and some crass—infringements on autonomy have resulted from negotiations for funding by foundations, federal agencies, and individual donors. Criticisms of university actions, student publications, or faculty statements by the American Legion, the Daughters of the American Revolution, and other groups have caused presidents and boards to take excessive punitive and preventive measures. Some organizations have sought status and professionalization by pressuring for and possibly subsidizing a special degree program (such as the group that gulled a university into offering a degree program in mobile homes by offer of a pittance).

The channels open to those who would restrict university autonomy depend somewhat upon their positions and their ethics. Some restrictions are actually forms of influence or persuasion, sometimes taking the form of bribes, threats, and appeals to higher authorities by individuals seeking a satisfactory course grade or some special treatment. In some cases this approach seems to have gained the desired results, but such crude villainy is certainly the exception. Misunderstanding and distrust of higher education sometimes are manifested by self-made men who have had few and perhaps unfortunate experiences with it. (One president occasionally remarked that faculty members might do well to recognize that those they fail often turn up later in the legislature.) In private and public life, some demagogues and bureaucrats view freedom in word or deed as perfidious and as evidence of the need for rigorous and rigid control. Television reporters and cameramen have in some cases employed their media to encourage violence and to hinder a university's attempts to explain the situation and to restore order. Pressure groups (political and social), by publicity releases or by calls to administrative officers, can make it exceedingly difficult for administrators, boards, legislators, faculty, or students to take a reasoned position and responsible action on troublesome issues. The natural tendency of the university administrator—recognizing the undesirable effect of bad publicity on resources—is to seek the resolution which will mute or avoid bad publicity and then delude himself that it was the right decision; faculty members, shielded by academic freedom and tenure, can afford to be less sensitive. Legislatures, state budget officers, and auditors may subtly influence (if not determine) patterns of expenditure just by the questions they raise and the data they demand as well as by informal criticisms and formal recommendations.

Other restrictions on autonomy take a more structured, rationalized form. Program budgeting is one technique that budget officers and legislative committees are using at present to try to understand a university and to relate dollars to specific programs. Approval of new programs and elimination of duplicative old ones have been functions of coordinating or control boards rather than of state offices or the legislature; coupled with a role restriction (as with the state colleges in California), these procedures can destroy autonomy at a very sensitive point. When (also in California state colleges) budgets are line item, the resulting rigidity almost ensures that no time will be available for creative thinking about major program revision or innovation.

State purchasing offices using preaudits to ensure that funds are available and authorized, that bids are taken, and that the cheapest available item is purchased constitute one of the most irritating forms of restriction. In Berdahl's dichotomy this restriction is procedural rather than substantive, but the department that cannot get instructional equipment and supplies for months or finds that some vital specification has been ignored may rightly feel that both substantive autonomy and academic freedom (professional competency) have been invaded.

Appeals to the courts from university policies and decisions have multiplied to the level where many presidents must seek legal counsel on almost every issue. Courts were formerly hesitant about intervening in university affairs but now seem concerned about due process in the university—perhaps reflecting public doubts about the university's capacity to handle its own affairs.

Faculty unions are still too recent in the university for their impact on autonomy to be assessed. One line of thought is that a union composed solely of research and instructional faculty will clear up the administrative role of departmental chairmen, deans, and other administrators, thus possibly increasing the autonomy of the university.

When universities began to provide service to society, they lost their elitist mystique. Their size and apparent wealth have encouraged many persons and groups to suspect, envy, and manipulate them. University expansionist dynamics have made it especially sensitive to pressures and vulnerable to attack. Today, pressures from inside and outside higher education are causing almost irresistible demands for restrictions on universities, their components, and their members. We must meet these demands by establishing a new balance between autonomy and constraint. Most of the new developments in higher education (for example, unionization, management systems, state or regional coordination, organizational changes) will have complex, multifarious effects, increasing autonomy in one area while constraining it in others. None of these factors will operate in isolation. Perhaps for that reason, new forms of cooperation must guide our actions just as new definitions of fundamentals must guide our thoughts.

CONCLUSIONS

Autonomy of the university, vis-à-vis the society of which it is a part, is not and cannot be absolute. Decisions at any level must take into account the university's goals and social responsibility.

Autonomy without responsibility and accountability is subject to erosion and retraction.

The normal state in regard to individuals and units within a university is interdependence rather than either complete dependence or complete autonomy.

Academic freedom involves a much narrower range of individual autonomy than faculty members are prone to believe.

Conflicts of interest as well as professionalism must be taken into account in defining autonomy.

3

Views about Autonomy
and Review

University autonomy can be just as effectively destroyed by the extension of undue autonomy to departments, colleges, individual professors, or the total faculty as by interference from outside. *The Confidence Crisis* documented that autonomous university departments have often tended to become preoccupied with graduate education and pure research to the detriment of undergraduate instruction, applied research, and public service. Most attempts made within the university to redress this imbalance of priorities focus on restricting departmental autonomy. Since many actions and pressures from external sources apparently directed at university autonomy actually are generated by departmental and faculty irresponsibility, external probing and pressure are sometimes welcomed by top administration as a means of recouping lost power.

Wolfle (1971) summarizes some of the developments that justify review and modification of departmental structures and operations:

The American university department has served science well; it has been a congenial unit, fostering esprit among its members and becoming the strongest unit in academic politics. . . .

But new conditions have arisen. . . . Most doctorates of the next two decades will not be employed by universities similar to those in which they earned their degrees; the majority will enter other kinds of work, for which a different educational preparation may be more suitable. The department has lived a useful life, but the time has come to honor its history and achievements with a ceremonial and sentimental retirement party.

In terms of public interest, the most urgent problems do not fit into departmental boundaries. Those multiplex problems require synthetic as well as analytic studies and call for close collaboration of scholars from several disciplines. . . .

In terms of science itself . . . departmental walls are no longer comfortable boundaries but have become barriers to the collaboration of scholars whose specialized knowledge and techniques defy traditional compartmentalization.

In terms of student interests, departmental boundaries are as much a nuisance as an aid to intellectual and vocational identification. Even at the Ph.D. level there is much field switching.

In terms of the university's ability to improve its own programs and to adapt constructively to the financial, political, and other pressures beating upon it, a strong case can be made that the principal centers of curricular, research, and planning responsibility should be fewer in number and broader in interest than the department.

Universities are under severe financial, political, and intellectual stress; disadvantageous as that stress is in other respects, it is in times of crisis that new procedures and organizational forms are likely to be accepted, for it is then that outworn habits are most easily broken.[1]

[1] Extracts from editorial used by permission of author, Dael Wolfle, and *Science* magazine.

Somewhat similarly, Koc (1971, p. 3) of the University of Lancaster in England remarks:

> We have a structure (heavily departmental) at variance with our professed teaching aims (multidisciplinary) and a collegiate system which is in danger of being reduced to a mere administrative device with petty responsibilities and no powers. Our statutes, created by culling bits from the statutes of other mediocre universities, contain no satisfactory mechanisms of adjustment to radically changed circumstances. . . . The feudal baronies created by some of the early professorial incumbents still set the tone to the place, with our local Napoleons still locked in battle for resources, influence, and student numbers so that they [can] pursue their peculiar glories unimpaired.

Both of these statements, though couched in different terms, suggest that the departmental organization poses a major impediment to achieving effective, flexible, and efficient university operation.

OPINION SURVEY

We undertook an opinion survey to gain further perspectives on the issue of university autonomy and decision-making responsibility. Implicit in the background of this survey were two assumptions about the contemporary American university. First, the department is likely to remain the basic unit for the operation and social organization of most universities. Second, the department's autonomy—like the university's—must be constrained by the needs and responsibilities of the institution and of the community in which it functions.

In this survey we sought to pursue the topic of institutional social responsibility by seeking opinions about appropriate levels for review of departmental decisions. We wanted to find answers to the following two questions: (1) Is there widespread acceptance of the need to review departmental actions? (2) What values or concerns justify the review?

We also wanted to see whether universities differ in these matters according to size, type of control, educational quality, or regional location. Accordingly, we selected forty-two universities located throughout the country, including several of those used in the previous study, to represent the various types of American universities. (Selection of the survey population is described in Appendix B.) Within each university, we chose nine departments and sent questionnaires to all their full-time faculty members. We also broadened the scope of the survey to include two other groups besides university faculty and administrators: legislators, since generally in the past few years they have sought to exert greater control over public universities; and governing board members, since they can determine a university's basic character and are sometimes underestimated as factors in the campus power structures. Although the response from these last two groups was considerably less than we had hoped for, it still allowed us to form some tentative conclusions about their attitudes.

We mailed questionnaires to approximately 10,000 faculty, 750 administrators, 650 board members, and 950 legislators concerned with education. The overall response rate for faculty was 40 per cent, or approximately 4,000 returns, varying from 20 per cent in some departments to almost 60 per cent in others. Response rates for administrators ranged even more widely, from zero in one university to 88 per cent, with an overall return of 45 per cent. Although differences in response rates among the nine disciplines were not significant, the highest response rates were in chemistry, botany (or biology), and management; lowest rates were in economics and mathematics; the rates for psychology, English, engineering, and history were in between. Responses from what are commonly regarded as "elite" universities were relatively low, as we had expected. *No* significant differences appeared in response rates by university size, region, and private or public control. (See Appendix B for a more complete analysis of response rates.)

The respondents in our survey cannot be viewed as a random sample drawn from all universities. We assume that those who responded share some of the authors' concerns about the present state of higher education, and we exhibit our results as indicative of the range of opinion.

We want our readers to be aware of the following: (1)

The subjects who responded might be biased in ways that could distort the results of our survey. (2) The response from legislators and board members was small in number and represents a small percentage of the survey population. (3) The pattern of response, as far as can be ascertained at this time, is consistent with that of *The Confidence Crisis*.

The questionnaire developed for this survey has three main sections. Findings from the first section and part of the third section are not directly relevant to the topics of this volume and therefore have been reported in other publications. (See facsimile of the questionnaire in Appendix A.) The second section of the questionnaire is concerned with the review of departmental actions. It contains a list of thirty-two actions or decisions typically undertaken by university departments. For each of these actions we asked each respondent to indicate the level—within an influence hierarchy of nine levels, ranging from individual faculty members to trustees and legislators—at which, in his opinion, the action *should* be reviewed; in other words, the highest level at which a veto could be legitimately exercised. (Respondents were also given the option "No review at all.")

Respondents were also asked to indicate the justification for the review of each action, choosing from a list of nine reasons. Undoubtedly, there are many reasons why a decision may be reviewed, and our questionnaire was designed to reveal the justifications that our respondents would accept as underlying a general review process.

The construction of any set of items such as these departmental decisions and the justifications for reviewing them is always subject to bias. There is no way of knowing whether the set of decisions we provided adequately represents the universe of decisions that might have been sampled, and the same is true of our set of justifications. Respondents might have opted for joint determination or consultation rather than review of decisions, but we allowed for no such opportunity. Judicious compromise may be the real world of academia, but we sought to uncover our respondents' ideal view of the review process and its justification.

Generally, the results of this survey were conservative. Differences among the four groups of respondents were relatively small and the overall pattern relatively close to what a well-informed observer would have predicted. From the results of the questionnaire we drew the following conclusions: (1) The four groups of respondents differ in their opinions of the appropriate level for review. (2) These differences are more salient on some issues than others. (3) The degree of difference among the four subgroups varies by issue. (4) Disagreements about appropriate review levels usually increase when one examines decisions ordinarily considered as administrative prerogatives. (5) Responses generally form a step pattern, with faculty members indicating the lowest level of review, followed by administrators, board members, and, finally, legislators, who usually select the highest level among the four groups. The legislators' responses on the average were one full level higher than faculty members'; the other two groups' responses fell between the extremes.

Levels of Review. In order to form a quantified index for the general levels of the review function perceived by the respondents, we arbitrarily assigned a numerical value to each possible hierarchical level, starting with a 1 for the individual faculty member and extending to 8 for legislatures. We then computed averages for each group's response to each specific item. The results, as given in Table 1, show, for example, that legislators believe that course reading assignments (item 9) are appropriately reviewed by the individual faculty member (level 1) but that decisions to change existing courses (item 26) should be reviewed by the department chairman or committees (level 2). Board members, administrators, and faculty chose about the same average ideal review level for these two items.

By retaining decimals, we could treat the hierarchy as a continuum rather than a set of discrete positions. For those who want names attached to these numbers, the midpoints become convenient breaking points. (For example, the range 2.51–3.50 could be considered *college* level; the range 1.51–2.50 *department* level.) However, the second line (for item 26) of average responses in Table 1 shows that the differences between the four

TABLE 1. LEVELS OF REVIEW

Departmental Actions in Order of Differences between Groups

	Average Response for Levels of Review			
	Leg.	Board	Adm.	Faculty
Very Little Difference between Groups [a]				
9. Course reading assignments	1.47 [b]	1.42	1.22	1.31
26. Changing existing course	2.62	2.45	2.58	2.35
28. Number & length of class meetings	3.09	2.86	3.31	2.93
6. Time of class meetings	3.32	3.09	3.24	2.84
Little Difference				
5. New course for nonmajors	3.69	3.26	3.36	3.05
17. Nonacademic personnel policies	5.33	5.39	5.09	4.77
30. Assigning teachers to courses	2.71	2.54	2.23	2.10
12. Contact hours assigned to faculty	3.48	3.23	3.05	2.80
3. Type of instruction	2.34	2.21	1.80	1.70
4. Class size	3.29	2.96	2.87	2.50
23. Admission criteria, graduate	3.68	3.32	3.19	2.88
15. Time for paid consulting	4.91	4.88	4.68	4.06
10. Adequacy & fairness of grading system	3.29	3.45	3.20	2.65
22. Faculty applications for research grants	4.08	3.94	3.79	3.20
Some Difference				
2. New undergraduate degree program	5.34	5.10	5.16	4.19
7. Course requirements	2.49	2.40	1.67	1.54
11. Use of computer	4.65	4.22	4.06	3.50
27. Number admitted, graduate students	3.80	3.51	3.14	2.71
1. New course, majors	3.84	3.71	3.24	2.78
Marked Difference				
8. New graduate degree program	5.84	5.53	5.37	4.52
21. Paid travel by faculty	3.71	3.08	2.59	2.49
13. Reduced teaching load for research	4.01	3.79	3.05	2.73
24. Selecting departmental chairman	4.41	4.30	3.71	3.05
20. Admission criteria, undergraduate	4.56	3.88	3.49	3.13
25. Faculty participation in governance	4.20	4.01	3.34	2.74
18. Tenure criteria	5.75	5.09	4.78	4.22
14. Faculty tenure appointment	5.24	5.06	4.60	3.70
Great Difference				
31. Student participation in department governance	4.11	4.05	2.94	2.72
29. Allocating departmental funds	4.56	4.16	3.55	2.98
16. Nonreappointing nontenured professor	4.72	4.15	3.41	3.12
32. Approving expenses for guest speakers, etc.	4.43	4.05	3.32	2.81

TABLE 1. LEVELS OF REVIEW—CONTINUED

	Average Response for Levels of Review			
	Leg.	Board	Adm.	Faculty
Very Great Difference				
19. Salaries for faculty	5.35	4.66	3.81	3.44
Average	4.01	3.74	3.40	2.98

a In order of increasing differences between groups. Items 10 and 22 have the same average difference between groups.

b Nine levels of review were listed for these items: 1—individual faculty member; 2—department; 3— college; 4—all-university faculty committees; 5—administration; 6—trustees or governing board; 7—central administration of a multicampus institution; 8—public officials or legislatures; 9—no review at all. Thus, the legislators' average response of 1.47 for item 9 indicates that most of the group chose the individual level as appropriate for reviewing course reading assignments; however, legislators' response of 2.62 for item 26 indicates that their response was closer to college level (3) than to department level (2).

groups of respondents are slight, even though the numeric values themselves indicate separate levels (legislators are near the third or college level, faculty members near the second or department level).

Faculty members apparently do not believe that they should always be the highest level of review. The sole area where most faculty members indicated that they should have final review rights—with complete agreement by the other three subgroups—was in reading assignments for a course. Thus, our data show no great desire by faculty members to engage in completely autonomous and personal behavior without review. Faculty members chiefly indicated the college level (23 per cent of their total responses) and department level (36 per cent) for the review function, as shown in Table 2.

Apparently, contrary to stereotypes, administrators are no more power hungry than the faculty. Administrators cited their own level in only 19 per cent of their responses, and they frequently put the review function at college level (31 per cent of administrators' responses) and department level (24 per cent).

Legislators generally put the review function at a higher

TABLE 2. LEVELS OF REVIEW

Average Per Cent of Responses at Each Level of Review,
by Four Main Groups of Respondents

Levels of Review	Legislators	Board Members	Admin- istrators	Faculty
1. Individual	6% a	5%	7%	11%
2. Department	17	20	24	36
3. College	22	25	31	23
4. All-university	9	10	10	12
5. Administration	24	27	19	11
6. Trustees	14	11	6	3
7. Multicampus administration	3	1	2	1
8. Public officials	3	—	—	—
9. No review at all	1	—	—	1

a Per cent of group's total response indicated for each review level.
NOTE: Chi-square test for population differences, using average per cent of responses at each level of review, shows the following: legislators-faculty, sig. at .01 level; board-faculty, sig. at .05 level; administrators-faculty, board-administrators, legislators-administrators, and legislators-board, *not* significant.

level than the on-campus respondents, but they rarely (only 3 per cent of their total choices) indicated the legislature as the proper review level. They chose the board level (14 per cent) a little more frequently than board members themselves did. They tended to choose the administration level (24 per cent) and college level (22 per cent) more than the departmental level (17 per cent). The board members' response pattern resembles the legislators' but with slightly more frequent choice of on-campus groups for review: administration (27 per cent), college (25 per cent), and department (20 per cent). Board members assigned almost no review functions to supracampus bodies such as a state-wide university system or legislature. Board members and legislators selected fewer lower levels for appropriate review than did faculty members or administrators. For only three items (3, 7, 9) did they both suggest that the review should be below the college level; both groups chose the all-university-committee level most often. In only two cases— tenure criteria and establishing new graduate degree programs

—did the legislators indicate that the board is the appropriate level. In short, legislators and board members did not allot the review function to themselves disproportionately.

Differences among the nine disciplines were slight in terms of their average levels of review, although the data suggest a pattern. (See also rate of return per discipline in Appendix B.) Average responses are as follows: mathematics, 3.09; management, 3.07; economics, 3.04; electrical engineering, 3.03; history, 2.99; English, 2.98; chemistry, 2.98; psychology, 2.86; biology, 2.76.

Apparently, biologists and psychologists want more of their activities reviewed at departmental level (or not at all) than do members of the other seven disciplines. We might surmise that biologists and psychologists are more collegial than the others, but many other factors also necessarily enter the picture. Without further data we cannot validly interpret these figures; for example, we would want to know more about the types of departments within each discipline. Since some disciplines tend to set the review authority outside the department more often than other disciplines, we could refer to a "conservative" group—from the faculty viewpoint—which would include mathematics, management, economics, and electrical engineering. English, history, and chemistry are only somewhat "conservative" in this sense. The more conservative group tended to differ from the less conservative group on certain activities; they indicated review levels higher than the faculty overall average for certain areas of departmental activities, as follows: adding or changing courses for majors and nonmajors; determining size, time, number, and length of classes; deciding tenure criteria, nonacademic personnel policies, and the firing of nontenured personnel; determining criteria for and number of graduate admissions; deciding about faculty participation in governance; determining such faculty perquisites as reduced teaching, paid consulting, and paid travel; and allocating departmental funds.

These findings suggest the sorts of activities on which more conservative faculty members take a more conservative position, but this pattern shows little correlation with the average degree of difference among disciplines concerning the review level for each particular activity.

When we checked the above data to ascertain differences by quality, size, and control, we found virtually no differences. Respondents at higher-prestige universities tended to place the review at levels below those indicated by respondents at lower-prestige universities; and also those at larger universities tended to select trustees as an appropriate review unit more than those at smaller ones. But these differences were not significant.

Justifications for Review. Besides indicating the level at which various departmental actions should be reviewed, respondents were asked to indicate principles that would justify reviewing departmental actions, choosing from a list of nine justifications. (See questionnaire facsimile, Appendix A.) As Table 3 shows, overall our respondents showed relatively high agreement on the justifications for review. Of the nine possible reasons provided, the justification most frequently chosen for all thirty-two items by all four groups was the efficient use of resources. This finding contradicts the notion in much popular literature that faculty members are unconcerned about effi-

TABLE 3. RANKINGS OF JUSTIFICATIONS FOR REVIEW

	Ranking by Respondent Groups (Frequency of Choice)			
Justifications for Review	Legislators	Boards	Administrators	Faculty
Efficient use of financial or human resources	1	1	1	1
Improved quality of education	2	2	2	2
Welfare of students	3	3	4	3
Uniform practice and policy in university	4	4	3	5
Welfare of total faculty	5	5	5	4
Academic freedom	6	6	6	6
Advancement of discipline or profession	7	7	7	7
Counterbalance to department's self-interest	8	8	8	8
Assigned role in a multi-campus stystem	9	9	9	9

ciency. The justification ranked second (but chosen much less frequently than efficiency) was improvement of the quality of education, upon which all four groups concur. Overall the respondents agreed on the top two justifications and the last four, while they disagreed on three in the middle. We were surprised by the amount of agreement because our campus interviews had revealed concern about lack of campus consensus.

Differences among the four groups' responses conform to what one would expect: faculty members cited faculty welfare and academic freedom more than did the other groups; more administrators cited efficiency. However, it is somewhat surprising that board members tended to use student welfare and educational quality as justifications slightly more than the other groups did. Administrators showed the greatest consensus of opinions; 45 per cent or more of them chose the same justification for twenty-one items, more than among the other three groups. Administrators showed a large consensus on twelve items, faculty members and board members on six, and legislators on three.

Table 4 shows some overall findings about levels of review and their justifications. The most frequently chosen reason, efficient use of resources, was selected in only 25 per cent of the total responses. Improvement in quality of education was chosen as a justification in less than 20 per cent of total responses. Table 4 shows that review of faculty salaries, irrespective of level of review chosen, is often justified by faculty welfare; review of the grading system is often justified by student welfare; and so on. "Counterbalancing departmental self-interest" and "advancing a profession or discipline" were rarely used as justifications, which suggests that these low-rated justifications are not clearly linked to any specific issues or areas of concern.

When we analyzed the data in terms of the seven disciplines in this study, we found that the disciplines of economics, management, and electrical engineering—which are more conservative in the sense of setting the review authority generally higher in the academic hierarchy—chose efficiency as a justification more often than the other disciplines. The less

TABLE 4. JUSTIFICATIONS FOR REVIEW

Department Actions Classified by Justification Cited for Review

Justifications	Total Number of Justifications, Per Cent	Departmental Actions for Which Justification was Cited [a]
Efficient use of resources	25	22. Faculty application for research grant 27. Number of graduate students admitted 19. Salaries for faculty 2. New undergraduate degree program 8. New graduate degree program 13. Reduced teaching load for research or service 4. Class size 12. Contact hours assigned to faculty 30. Assigning teachers to courses 21. Paid travel by faculty 32. Approving expenses for guest speakers, etc. 6. Time of class meetings 17. Nonacademic personnel policies 29. Allocating departmental funds 11. Use of computer
Improvement in quality of education	19	16. Nonreappointing nontenured faculty 7. Course requirements 2. New undergraduate degree program 3. Type of instruction 28. Number, length of class meetings 5. New course for nonmajors 20. Admission criteria for undergraduates 1. New course for majors 26. Changing an existing course
Welfare of students	15	4. Class size 20. Admission criteria for undergraduates 23. Number of undergraduates admitted to department 31. Student participation in department governance 10. Grading system

TABLE 4. JUSTIFICATIONS FOR REVIEW—CONTINUED

Justifications	Total Number of Justifications, Per Cent	Departmental Actions for Which Justification was Cited [a]
Welfare of total faculty	11	14. Faculty tenure appointment 24. Selecting departmental chairman 19. Salaries for faculty 25. Faculty participation in governance
Uniform practice in a university	10	18. Tenure criteria 15. Time for paid consulting by faculty 17. Nonacademic personnel policies
Academic freedom	8	3. Type of instruction 7. Course requirements 9. Course reading assignments
Advancement of a discipline or profession	5	22. Faculty applications for research grants [b] 13. Reduction in teaching for research or service [b]
Counterbalance to department interests	3	24. Selecting departmental chairman [b]
Assigned role in a multicampus system	1	

[a] For each of these actions, at least 26 per cent of total choices for justifications was for the justification listed at left. Actions are listed within sections in order of percentage of total response for each item given to justification at left; i.e., efficiency was used more frequently to justify reviewing item 22 (faculty application for research grant) than for reviewing item 11 (use of computer). Some actions have several justifications.

[b] Fewer than 25 per cent of total responses for this action were indicated for the justification listed at left.

conservative disciplines (biology, chemistry, English, history, psychology) tended to choose educational quality, academic freedom, and student welfare as justifications slightly more often than the former group. Since the differences between disciplines were mostly small, these findings are more thought-provoking than significant.

When we related the average level of review for each item with the percentage of responses per justification for the same items, we found certain levels of review generally associated with certain justifications: when respondents chose review at the board or the administration level, they frequently cited uniformity as justification; when they chose the administration level, they cited efficiency; all-university groups as a level was accompanied by educational quality or efficiency as justification; the college level was frequently justified by faculty welfare, student welfare, educational quality, or efficiency; and the departmental or individual level was justified by academic freedom.

Faculty respondents were not unanimous in their selection of review levels, and these vary by the goals or issues involved, as would be true of the other four groups as well. But certain levels and certain justifications were seldom used together. For example, faculty did not consider review by the administration as a means for advancing educational quality, promoting faculty or student welfare, or preserving academic freedom. In the minds of faculty the issues, levels of review, and justifications are linked together into a complex set of alternatives. Although we could not analyze all of the data in this manner, we are sure that the other three respondent groups have equivalent interrelationships.

Apparently respondents had certain concerns in mind when they indicated various justifications for reviewing departmental actions. We interpreted justifications as indications of certain needs felt by respondents regarding particular departmental actions. About 45 per cent of the administrators selected uniformity to justify reviewing the time allowed for paid consulting by the faculty and nonacademic personnel policies, which indicated to us that administrators felt a need for uniformity in those two activities. More than half of the administrators and faculty members apparently felt a need for efficiency in scheduling the time of class meetings. About two thirds of all respondents showed concern that computer services, allocations of departmental funds, and nonacademic personnel policies should be reviewed with regard to efficiency; that is, they felt a need for efficiency in those areas. Among administrators and faculty members, about half chose "student welfare" as justification for review of the grading system; and they chose "academic freedom" as justification for review of reading assignments (or for their belief that reading assignments require no review).

No differences in justifications selected were related to any of our control variables—size, region, type of control, or prestige.

Opinions about University Operations. In the final section of the questionnaire (see Appendix A) respondents were provided with seventeen opinions about university operations and were asked to indicate their level of agreement with each. In general we found slight differences among our four groups. (A Kruskal-Wallis test applied to the groups' average levels of agreement per item showed no significant differences between groups. A chi-square test applied to the average per cent of responses at each level of agreement showed no significant differences between groups.) Nor were there marked differences when institutional variables were introduced. Apparently our respondents have a general consensus about these statements. Table 5 shows the average levels of agreement and the pattern of differences for these data.

The respondents' overall reaction to these statements is more middle-of-the-road than one might have expected. About a third of the respondents indicated only *some* agreement with about a third of the statements. Many respondents took middle-of-the-road positions where one might have expected an extreme reaction: among faculty members 42 per cent showed *some* agreement that a department's inefficiency justifies incursions into autonomy (item 10) and 26 per cent showed *great* agreement; 53 per cent showed only *some* agreement or less with the position that departmental autonomy is essential for highest-quality education (item 12). Among legislators 57 per cent indicated only *some* or less agreement that universities are trying to do more than their resources can support (item 13).

TABLE 5. STATEMENTS OF OPINION

In Order of Differences between Groups

Statements of Opinion	Average Level of Agreement [b]			
	Leg.	Board	Admin-istrators	Faculty
Very Little Difference between Groups [a]				
11. Legistlatures have right to set minimum instructional loads for faculty.	1.13	1.09	1.03	.97
Little Difference				
9. If faculty were more attentive to instructional problems, student pressure on administrations would lessen.	2.31	2.44	2.22	1.90
13. Universities generally are trying to do more than their available resources can support.	2.26	2.65	2.89	2.64
3. University autonomy is essential to preserve intellectual creativity.	2.32	2.94	2.90	2.97
6. A major reason for infringing on university autonomy lies in the lack of understanding of educational matters by laymen.	1.60	2.00	2.01	2.27
10. Incursions into a department's autonomy are justified when a department operates inefficiently.	2.82	2.74	2.57	2.13
16. Faculty usually tries to increase research time at the expense of time that should be spent on teaching.	2.40	2.32	2.12	1.79
1. Infringements on departmental autonomy imply a denial of professional competency.	1.40	1.15	1.11	1.77
12. Departmental autonomy is essential to ensure highest quality of education.	1.58	1.67	1.58	2.31
14. A very high degree of specialization by professors requires universities to limit departmental autonomy.	1.61	1.69	1.50	.96
7. Basic conflicts of interest between departments and their university require monitoring by others outside university.	1.20	.72	.40	.56
8. Dept. chairman's role should include protecting his faculty against infringements on department autonomy.	1.82	1.84	1.85	2.72

TABLE 5. STATEMENTS OF OPINION—CONTINUED

	Average Level of Agreement [b]			
	Leg.	Board	Admin-istrators	Faculty
Some Difference				
17. Operation of the university should be turned over to faculty.	.38	.19	.36	1.22
4. Incursions into a university's autonomy are justified when a university operates inefficiently.	2.83	2.37	2.06	1.81
2. Departments exist to carry out university policy.	2.15	2.30	1.72	1.29
5. Governing boards must establish minimum teaching loads to insure that professors are in the classroom.	1.82	1.57	.84	.86
Marked Difference				
15. University administrators do not exert enough control over faculty work load.	2.01	2.05	1.65	.61
Average	1.86	1.87	1.69	1.69

[a] Within sections, items are in order of increasing difference between groups. Items with same average difference are bracketed.

[b] These figures represent the average of responses by each group. Five levels of agreement were listed for these items: $0 =$ none, $1 =$ slight, $2 =$ some, $3 =$ great, $4 =$ very great. Legislators' average response of 1.40 for item 1 indicates that most legislators agree slightly with the statement.

Several of the responses were surprising. Fully half of the legislators agreed to a *great* or *very great* extent that university autonomy is essential to intellectual creativity (item 3). All groups strongly disagreed (administrators most of all) that conflicts between a university and its departments require monitoring from outside (item 7). Also, all groups strongly disagreed (at almost identical rates) that legislatures have the right to set teaching loads at public universities (item 11). The strongest reaction overall was to the statement that the university's operation should be turned over to the faculty: board members disagreed emphatically (88 per cent), but even most faculty members were against it (60 per cent).

By intercorrelating the statements, we located clusters along two dimensions: autonomy and intervention. Items 1, 3, 6, 8, and 11 reflect the autonomy factor. Items 4, 5, 9, 11, 14, 15, and 16 reflect the intervention factor.

The correlations in the autonomy cluster suggest that agreement with the statement "Departmental autonomy is essential to ensure highest quality of education" is central for this cluster. Those who agree with that statement tend also to consider infringements upon autonomy as a denial of professional competence and to believe that a chairman's role is to protect the faculty. Our pattern of correlations suggests that department chairmen have functions to protect the faculty on two grounds. One is related to quality of education when infringements deny professional competency; and the other is related to laymen's intervention, which might curtail intellectual creativity.

In the intervention cluster, agreement with the statement "University administrators do not exert enough control over faculty work load" is central and correlates highly with the statement "A very high degree of specialization by professors requires universities to limit departmental autonomy." Both specialization and the faculty's increased research time are correlated with the lack of administrator control over work loads. The latter is also correlated with statements that governing boards and legislators should set minimum standards for the faculty.

CONCLUSIONS

Near the beginning of this chapter we stated two questions which we hoped to answer in the course of our analysis: (1) Is there widespread acceptance of the need to review departmental actions? (2) What values or concerns justify the review? After studying the data from our survey, we think that we now have sufficient evidence to suggest some tentative answers.

Many people connected with universities accept the need for a review of departmental actions. But this review is generally thought to be best handled by persons or groups within the university, usually by faculty or by administrators at various levels. The review process is viewed somewhat differently by legislators, governing board members, administrators, and faculty members; but on the whole we were impressed with the amount of agreement among these groups. In our sample, legislators and board members do not exhibit strong desires to take on the task of reviewing the major portion of departmental operations. Administrators also seem wary of assuming a major role in review. A majority of faculty members think that many departmental operations should be reviewed by persons outside the department; and a sizable minority believe that certain departmental decisions should be reviewed at the administration level or above. Ultimately, cases of *who* reviews *what* can be settled only in the actual situation at particular institutions. No general pattern based on institutional size, prestige, region, or type of control seems to apply.

The values underlying our respondents' views seem more pragmatic and rational than one might expect. Efficiency, uniformity, a better "product"—these appear to be major concerns in universities. But humane concerns—personal and intellectual welfare—are not neglected, especially on particular issues. Our data suggest that stereotypic criticisms of faculty members as overidealistic or administrators as overbureaucratic do not fit the contemporary university. The results of our survey appear to us conservative in the current higher education scene, but also progressive in the sense that they manifest a balance between self-interest and social responsibility that is essential for the rejuvenation of American universities. Yet we remain concerned by the hostile comments we received from some respondents and the apparent disregard or antagonism of the many who failed to respond. To judge by our respondents, questions of autonomy, review, and constraint can arouse great rage and anxiety in some members of the higher education community. Whether this inclination is the reaction of a noisy but innocuous minority or of many embittered academics, we naturally do not know. But we are more than ever aware of the portentous nature of these topics.

4

New Patterns
of Organization

The operations of universities are often rigidified by their traditional patterns of organization. In the United States, the prevalent pattern is some combination of a basic structure of colleges and/or schools, subdivided into departments and supplemented by a loose and varied array of institutes, centers, offices, bureaus, and program coordinating committees. Difficulties in attaining any comprehensive reorganization of the basic structure or even a fundamental reorganization in units of that basic structure usually have led to one of two alternatives: (1) addition of new units, including new colleges or departments but more often the ubiquitous institutes or centers; (2) reorganization (and usually expansion) of central administration by inserting new levels or by introducing more specialization in administrative assignments.

The first alternative (new units) further complicates the

structure and multiplies the problems of coordination, governance, and budgeting. The second (reorganization), often proposed as a means of clarification and simplification, too frequently becomes an exercise in futility wherein the stated rationale is unclear or even deliberately misleading and the results ineffective or even chaotic.

This chapter discusses briefly some examples of reorganization as well as the organization of some new institutions. The background for writing this chapter included visits to a number of new universities in England, where the rationale for organizational pattern is clear and the success of developments over a period of time is becoming evident. It also included visits to fifteen institutions (some new and some recently reorganized) in the United States, where the rationale is frequently less clear and the recency of developments leaves the future uncertain. Since administrators in several of these institutions expressed a preference for anonymity, descriptive pseudonyms have been used for all United States institutions.

In these new institutions, it became evident that an administrator selected to launch a new institution can, in the absence of any faculty or student body, create an organization based on an elaborate rationale or simply mold it to his own preferences. How well this organization functions and whether it can survive the pressures toward a more traditional pattern are questions of significant import. With the exception of some few reorganizations based on whims and idiosyncrasies of administrators or adjustments to accommodate difficult personalities or incompetents, both the reorganization of mature institutions and the initial organization of new institutions have, in recent years, been based upon similar fundamental concerns.

BASIC CONCERNS IN INNOVATION ORGANIZATIONS

Perhaps foremost among the concerns giving rise to new patterns of organization is concern about undergraduate education. This concern is prominent in the remarks of administrators (presidents or chancellors in this country and vice chancellors in Britain) who have been charged with the devel-

opment of a new institution. That this concern is widely shared
by other faculty members and administrators is demonstrated
by the ease with which sympathetic faculty, deans, and provosts
are recruited for new institutions. Other factors—such as more
rapid promotion and the exhilaration of being in on the formative stage of a new institution—influence recruitment, to be
sure; but interviews at a number of these new institutions con-
clusively document that dissatisfaction with traditional
programs and the challenge of a new approach are strong
motivations for established senior academics to move to a new
scene.

Innovators' concern about undergraduate instruction
has at least four facets. One is a conviction that the usual
organization into disciplinary-related departments is inimical
to sound undergraduate education. Avoidance of departments
at the University of Wisconsin at Green Bay, the University of
California at Santa Cruz, and the universities of Sussex, Kent,
and East Anglia in England illustrates the point. A second facet
is the belief that the student should be given a broad though
interrelated experience with several disciplines, which the departmental structure does not readily provide. This sort of
program requires interdisciplinary courses taught by professors
of broad scholarship or a coordinated team of professors representing different disciplines. The third facet is the concept of
relevance, implying the need for courses that center on current
issues or social problems and that also appeal to students and
enhance their career opportunities (by providing study in
usable depth of several disciplines rather than concentration on
a single one). The fourth facet of concern about undergraduate
instruction is the expectation that the college experience ought
to provide something more than courses and an increase in
formal knowledge. This concern leads to an organization that
offers more meaningful social interactions among a group of
students and faculty members, some opportunity for students
to participate in planning their own education, and sufficient
flexibility so that individuals can explore various alternatives
and adjust their programs as their interests and self-images
change and mature. Implicit in this concern is a general aware-

ness of the affective and character-development aspects of education, which are largely ignored in the departmentally developed curriculum. An attempt to overcome the sense of isolation and dehumanization, which besets many students on large university campuses, dictates an organization that assures the student some continuing contacts with other students and faculty.

Another major concern among innovators is the faculty. The departmental structure encourages overspecialization as each faculty member seeks to develop his own specialty, both in his research and in his teaching. Isolated in his department, the professor has little incentive and no opportunity to consider the totality of undergraduate education and the varying interests and aspirations of individual students. To meet this problem, an organization is sought in which professors will have some informal contact with students outside of courses, and those with interests extending beyond their specialty can organize and teach courses of a broader orientation (perhaps interdisciplinary or problem-oriented). Particularly needed is a surer means of recognizing and rewarding excellent teaching, whether or not accompanied by research output. Intertwined with these concerns is a feeling that departmental affiliations breed loyalty to the discipline and perhaps to the department, but seldom to the institution. An organization that encourages the individual instructor to view the institution as a whole and to become involved in its larger purposes has been a goal in a number of new institutions.

Junior faculty members have a limited voice in many departments, and yet there is nowhere else in the university where they can be heard. Undoubtedly that is why many of the younger faculty members have been sympathetic to student activists and have offered them assistance in embarrassing or constraining the establishment. Patterns of organization which provide the junior faculty member with an opportunity to assert his views and express his individuality have been sought in several of the new institutions.

A third area of concern essential to understanding new organizations combines pressures for accountability and for stronger administrative control. There are two reasons for this concern. New institutions, especially public-supported ones, are quite cost-conscious; usually their costs must not exceed those of more traditional institutions, and they must carefully account for the resources assigned them. Administrators are ever conscious of this. In addition, the administrators of a new institution has probably planned—at least in broad sweep—the curriculum; the buildings; the major purposes, themes, or emphases; and even the patterns of interaction of students, faculty, and administration. He does not readily relinquish his vision, and he seeks in various ways (not always obvious to himself) to maintain authority sufficient to ward off abrupt changes. The more gradual and inevitable erosions of the original grand scheme are less perceptible to the founder, and may be unrecognized or denied after they are apparent to staff and to even casual observers.

The administration necessarily plays a dominating role in the early stages of new institutions. An organization that eschews traditional structures (with widely accepted expectations of autonomy in curriculum, research, and budgeting) in favor of new structures (such as interdisciplinary schools, theme colleges, and broad faculty groupings) also assures a formative period in which roles and prerogatives are unclear, and the tendency will be to look to the top for direction. Almost any atypical innovative structure creates this situation. Whether the initial pattern can remain viable in the face of increasing size, complexity, and faculty and student attempts to modify a structure which they did not form and which, to them, has no mystique is one of our central questions.

NEW ORGANIZATIONS IN ENGLAND

University of Sussex. The University of Sussex, at Brighton, is organized into nine "studies" groups, or schools. To "avoid cutting off from one another subjects that could and should be usefully drawn together" (*Guide for Applicants, 1969–70*, p. 10), there are no departments. The Arts and Social Studies schools are African and Asian Studies, Cultural and Community Studies, English and American Studies, European Studies, and Social Sciences. The Science schools are Applied

Sciences, Biological Sciences, Mathematical and Physical Sciences, and Molecular Sciences. Additional schools are under consideration, but existing schools tend to resist new schools because of dilution of resources. They would prefer to add any new programs to existing schools, despite associated problems of size, maintenance of flexibility, and retention of the theme or character.

Every faculty member is associated with a school, but scholars in the same subject field may belong to different schools. Informal subject "committees" provide for discussions and advice and some coordination of courses, selection of new faculty, and other matters commonly handled by departments. The Sciences, because of their laboratories and their specialized interests, approximate a departmental organization; and their schools are more clearly disciplinary-oriented than the Social Studies and Arts schools. Every undergraduate belongs to one of the schools, which provides both academic life and social center for students and faculty, who cooperate in running school affairs.

The chief feature of the Sussex undergraduate course is its combination of specialist studies with work in related fields. The undergraduate follows a preliminary course in his school during the first two terms. In addition to his major-subject courses, he takes additional courses, called *contextual courses,* in the Arts and Social Studies and *supporting courses* in the Sciences. For example, an undergraduate major in English takes contextual courses of historical, philosophical, or sociological nature to help him understand English literature in its intellectual and social context. The undergraduate spends approximately half to two thirds of his time preparing for his final examination in his major subject, the remainder being given to the contextual or supporting courses.

Although administrative officers report that this scheme is popular with students, Perkin (1969, pp. 119, 84) reports:

> Students we interviewed were against it, pointing to the frequent reviews and reappraisals which have prevented it from settling down.

The member of staff may have even less firm anchorage

in this structure. . . . He will now belong either, as generally on the science side, to a single, large, amorphous "super-department" (as one Sussex science dean described it) or, as is common on the arts side, at one and the same time to two, three, or even more overlapping schools.

The school plan does provide considerable flexibility in that students can retain several options for at least a year, and they can even switch from one school to another within the Arts–Social Studies group or the Science group. Changes from Arts–Social Studies to Science are difficult and unlikely, but changes in the other direction do occur.

Aside from titles, the Sussex administrative pattern emerges as very similar to the American pattern of president, several vice-presidents, deans of colleges, and chairmen of departments. Some persons at Sussex knowledgeable of the usual university pattern in the United States regard it as equivalent. There is a strong probability that all scholars in a single subject will shortly be placed in one school and be treated as a department, whatever the terminology. The budgeting and planning procedure, as described, seems also to be moving closer to this pattern, although in earlier years schools were apparently the starting point for budget.

University of Essex. The teaching and research buildings of the University of Essex, at Colchester, form a continuous zigzag. The single continuous structure permits the assigning of contiguous locations to departments with related interests. The eleven departments and centers of the university are grouped into four overlapping schools, which provide groups of interrelated studies but do not have separate faculties. The aim is to have a balanced academic community with a range of disciplines over the entire spectrum but not attempting to include all of them. The compactness of the design makes central features, such as the lecture-theatre block, the computing center, and the language laboratories, easily accessible to all departments.

The schools and departments at Essex are interrelated as indicated in Figure 1.

FIGURE 1

RELATIONS OF SCHOOLS AND DEPARTMENTS
UNIVERSITY OF ESSEX [a]

School   *Department*

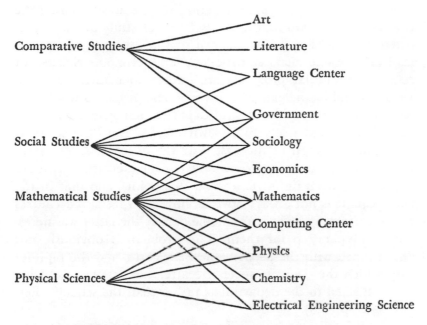

[a] University of Essex *1971–72 Prospectus,* p. 7.

Most departments are related to at least two schools, and four are related to three schools.

The first-year schemes in the four schools are broad enough to permit students the widest possible leeway in choosing second- and third-year schemes. If a student comes to the university knowing the subject he wishes to study for three years and to take for his honors degree, he is able to choose the first-year scheme that best suits his interests and qualifications. A student who is undecided (because, for instance, some subjects were not taught at his secondary school), or who changes his mind during the first year, has considerable freedom of choice in his final degree subject.

Second- and third-year schemes of study also cover more than one discipline. For example, the second- and third-year program in mathematical economics is offered jointly by the departments of mathematics and economics. Three types of courses are offered both in the second and third years: mathematics and statistics, economics, and bridge courses relating the two. Graduates who follow this scheme of study are well prepared for careers in government or private enterprise as mathematicians, economists, statisticians, and econometricians, or researchers. Similar programs are offered in mathematics and sociology and mathematical politics. These programs would not readily be provided in a typical departmental structure, where each is interested solely in its own majors. But "the students complain that even in the first year the different subjects are not tied in together and continuously compared (though there has recently been improvement on this point), and that in the later years it is not always obvious how the specialized courses follow on from the first-year scheme or why the latter was necessary as preparation for them. The problem is obviously not unconnected with the departmental structure, and the rapidity with which the students specialize after the first year and become attached to the department rather than the school" (Perkin, 1969, p. 123).

University of Kent. The University of Kent, at Canterbury, is organized into faculties akin to the schools at Sussex. The titles of the faculties at Canterbury (Humanities, Natural Sciences, Mathematical Studies, and Social Sciences), however, are more directly related to the disciplines or groups of disciplines than the theme titles of some of the Sussex schools.

Part I (the initial phase) of each area of study is wider than the conventional single subject. It includes a group of related disciplines in a deliberately integrated approach, covering fundamental principles and essential connections between disciplines as a foundation for the more specialized study in Part II. Work in Part II involves specialization of the usual kind— often in a single subject, sometimes in prescribed combinations of subjects. All courses at Canterbury are coordinated by boards of studies (or committees) responsible for course and examination requirements and for providing advice to students in the combination programs.

Kent also is organized into colleges, which are primarily student residences; but to promote intermingling of faculty and students, faculty members are assigned offices in the colleges. The collegiate organization is an essential feature of the university. Every student, graduate or undergraduate, becomes a member of one of the colleges of the university. The college provides a focus for a common life in which all its members share and to which they can develop real loyalties. Each college is diverse enough to achieve effective everyday contact between students and staff in different disciplines.

Although Kent has no formal departments, all its programs include traditionally named subjects and its faculty members are listed by discipline groups. Expansion in size is altogether likely to force recognition of a de facto departmental structure.

Students have a fairly high degree of flexibility at Canterbury, but those who move toward an interfaculty program face some problems. In theory, boards of studies rather than departments provide guidance and contacts for them; in practice, these students are lost souls, compared with those in the single-subject concentration, which provides a definite home.

University of East Anglia. The academic program at the University of East Anglia, at Norwich, is another effort to avoid excessive specialization. It attempts to break down departmental barriers by incorporating two or more traditional subjects into the student's program. The university is organized into a number of broadly based Schools of Studies: Biological Sciences, Chemical Sciences, English and American Studies, Environmental Sciences, European Studies, Fine Arts and Music, Mathematics and Physics, and Social Studies. School programs replace what otherwise would be departmental single-subject programs. The School of Environmental Sciences, for example, focuses on the study of the earth in all its aspects. The school draws upon the methods of mathematics, physics, chemistry, and biology, as well as upon geography, geology and geophysics, oceanography, meteorology, hydrology, soil science,

ecology, and urban and regional planning. The school finds
advantages in this broad coverage, since techniques used in one
course are applicable in others, and the same numerical methods
can be applied to many different kinds of data.

The School of European Studies offers courses in the
history, literature, and languages of Europe since the Renais-
sance. All students follow a common program during the first
two terms. Later they may concentrate on either history or
literature; but whichever field they choose, they continue with
the other or combine their major field with one or more subjects taught in other schools. The choice is to some extent limited by aptitude, previous training, and by certain requirements
aimed at preventing undue specialization, but it is not restricted
by a student's qualifications or his preference on entry to the
university.

The university places special emphasis on the problems
of developing countries. The programs provide rigorous training in one of several disciplines, but also combine that discipline with other subjects so that students will attain special
knowledge and understanding of the nature and problems of
developing countries. Thus, a student majoring in economics
may combine this discipline with relevant courses in sociology,
social anthropology, history, or environmental sciences.

The school is viewed as a teaching and social unit and
also as an effective base for integration of studies and the development of interdisciplinary programs. Nevertheless, school
barriers tend to replace departmental ones, and faculty members unsympathetic to the particular interdisciplinary patterns
embraced by the schools find it difficult to develop alternative
patterns. A traditional discipline usually exists in only one
school and combinations cutting across schools are not easily
arranged. Flexibility and deferred choice are available to students within a school, but transfers from one school to another
are rather difficult.

Doubts are widely prevalent at East Anglia that the
school structure is an appropriate vehicle for expansion to
10,000 students. Doubling the size of the schools would jeopardize the present size advantage. Any expansion in the number

of schools is viewed with some distaste because resources would have to be divided among more units and because the basic disciplines would almost certainly appear in more than one school. Those who would prefer a departmental structure see duplicating of disciplinary units as distinctly undesirable and would prefer to move directly to departments, with schools becoming more analogous to the college in the usual American university. Twin schools of the present variety are also rejected. From the viewpoint of the faculty, the question is how to organize when the number of historians, language specialists, and the like, becomes two or three times the present number. The present pattern of organization is under strain; how it will develop is uncertain.

Other English Universities. The large urban universities tend to be heavily departmentalized, although they have made efforts in the direction of more flexibility by developing combined honors and even general honors programs. One vicechancellor in an urban university characterized the departments as empires ruled by the chairman or professor, with these chairmen collectively dominating university decisions and effectively protecting their own interests by thwarting innovation.

Lancaster is a departmental university that aims at breadth throughout the degree. Qualified students have a choice between two or more major courses after their first year of study. *Depth* is provided by allowing considerable specialization in a major subject or a group of combined major subjects. *Balance* is attained by the inclusion of either a minor course closely related to the major interest or at least one other major subject. *Breadth* is acknowledged by inclusion of an additional course delving into a subject and method of thought different from the student's major interests.

In Part I of each program, the student takes three subjects of equal weight: his intended major (or majors) and a cognate field. In Part II, the student may major in any one of these subjects (or continue with two or even all three as a joint major). He need not make a final decision on his main specialty until the end of the first year. In Part II, occupying the second and third years, he may spend two thirds of his time (six units out of nine) on his major subject; two ninths on a cognate minor, such as politics or English for historians or computer science for mathematicians; and the remaining ninth on a second-year "distant minor" or "breadth subject," such as, for historians, a course in mathematics or science. A joint-major student spends four ninths of his time on each of his majors, plus either the breadth subject or a cognate subject. Triple-major students spend a third of their time on each subject and are deemed to have fulfilled the breadth requirement. There are pressures for more specialization and broader definition of the breadth component.

Three university charters (Keele, Sussex, and Kent) refer to Faculties, but only the last uses that term in practice. The other new universities manage their academic affairs (below the level of senate) through schools or boards of studies. Perkin's (1969, p. 145) views on this pattern are relevant to our concerns.

> The schools in particular, in spite of the overlapping membership, seem to consist of a core of subject specialists, committed to a certain view of the educational objectives, who tend to resist the introduction of new and "extraneous" subjects and especially the modification of the common courses. The boards of studies are more flexible and can more readily accommodate new subjects, but only at the expense of fragmenting into the departmentalism of the traditional faculty.
>
> Departmentalism, in fact, is the besetting sin of the academic profession, whether in the old or the new universities. It is easy to see why it should be so: a university teacher has invested an enormous intellectual and educational capital in his specialized subject, and to allow changes in or encroachment upon it by other specialists represents a threat to "property," which could render the investment obsolete and the specialist redundant, if not intellectually destitute.

A number of the new universities, in the attempt to avoid departmentalization, have made special efforts to develop interdisciplinary teaching. One variety is the interdisciplinary lecture course, in which lecturers from different disciplines follow but do not interact with each other. A second variety uses tutors in disciplines different from that of the lecturer in discussions with groups of students of issues arising in the lectures. A third brings together tutors from different disciplines who jointly discuss a topic with a group of students. The fourth variety brings students from different disciplines to the same discussion groups, with the expectation that their different orientations will evoke spirited discussion and new insights.

Perkin's (1969, p. 177) comments echo experiences in the United States: "The general conclusion would seem to be that there is less real interdisciplinary—that is, joint—teaching in the new universities than one might have expected from their educational aims and philosophies. Almost everywhere many of the staff and most of the students claimed that they would like more of it, but in practice the staff found it hard and sometimes unrewarding work and the students were often disappointed with the specific interdisciplinary lecture courses which they attended, though they were more enthusiastic about some of the jointly taught seminars."

NEW AND REORGANIZED UNIVERSITIES IN THE UNITED STATES

The American institutions selected for study did not constitute a systematic sample; they were selected simply because each was known to have developed an innovative organization. Only a few of those visited are explicitly discussed here. They have been selected to exemplify an organization and the rationale for it and to present some critique or analysis of its apparent effectiveness in overcoming some of the weaknesses of departmental organization.

South Coastal State University. South Coastal State University is an upper-level university in the state university system. Students are admitted after two years of undergraduate study elsewhere, chiefly in the public junior colleges. The university is expected, in time, to develop graduate degree programs in most areas, but temporary restraints have been placed upon this development. The university is committed to developing a highly individualized educational experience for its students and to integrating research activities into the teaching function. The plan emphasizes curricular flexibility, residential college structure (although only 12 per cent of the students live on campus), and the opportunity for directed study in each discipline.

The organization and the curriculum are based on traditional disciplinary patterns but include the possibility of interdisciplinary programs. The colleges present an unusual aggregation of disciplines. College 1 includes English and theater arts; psychology, sociology, anthropology, and social science; mathematics and statistics; marketing; and special and professional education. College 2 includes history, music, philosophy, religion, Latin American studies, and interdisciplinary humanities (a strong humanities orientation), as well as chemistry, biological and marine sciences, accounting and finance, elementary education, physical education, health, and recreational education. College 3 includes art and foreign languages, economics and political science, physics, business administration and management, aeronautical systems and systems science, and vocational-technical education.

Colleges have their own facilities but are related so as to assure overall harmony and efficiency. Students and faculty are assigned to the college that includes their major discipline. There is to be no duplication of academic programs among the colleges, and the student may take courses offered in other colleges so long as they are appropriate to his goals. Typically, a student might take about two thirds of his academic work in his own college and about one third elsewhere.

The following major advantages are claimed for the program: (1) The student lives and does most of his academic work in a setting much like that of a good small liberal-arts college, but has available the total academic resources of the university. (2) Students and faculty live and work closely with others who represent a broad variety of academic fields. They do not, however, lose the benefits produced by rigorous specialization in a particular discipline. (3) The resident colleges are reasonably comparable to each other and are of reasonable size. The college provost is responsible for the overall life and work of the college, not solely its academic administration. (4) Interdisciplinary and intercollege programs are encouraged and facilitated.

(5) Planning is improved because of the constraint placed upon the size of the resident college. The ultimate size of the university (five residential colleges of two thousand students each) is viewed as not exceeding thirteen thousand students. This includes some three thousand students for graduate professional programs, such as law and medicine, which do not fit the residential college structure.

A number of problems arise. As is true in most innovative institutions, many of the original faculty saw an exciting new challenge and an opportunity to advance faster. Reality imposes unforeseen limitations.

One problem arises out of the state system's requirements and practices. The timetable of SCSU (eighty-minute classes, with Wednesday afternoon kept open for faculty meetings and student-group meetings) differs from that of the rest of the system. This variant schedule has to be reconciled with state space and cost study requirements. The state system is frustrated when three deans from SCSU attend meetings of business school deans.

Provosts of the three colleges see themselves as miniature presidents. They have their own departments, courses, students, student government, and newspaper and are concerned with buildings, grounds, plant, and maintenance problems for their own village. But this whole concept is now being called into question on practical grounds. Students find that three student presidents, three student newspapers, and many small dormitories present such an administrative morass that it is difficult for them to reach the administration. They feel isolated from the administration rather than closer to it. Since each provost deals with a motley of disciplines (and is regarded as not understanding most of them), department chairmen push toward a university solution. Some chairmen indicate that several department chairmen and at least three provosts must agree in order to solve their problems.

The university is now questioning and examining the original organizational pattern. Many people have concluded that the organizational pattern will hold only as long as the original president remains in office. Though one may discount this as a common remark wherever innovation is associated with the chief executive officer, strong departmental pressures are at work at this university to force a more traditional pattern. The organizational pattern has not displaced the department as the major unit of organization; it has only diluted the composite strength of departments by an atypical grouping. If and when the graduate program is permitted to grow, and especially when doctoral programs are added, it is easy to predict that the interests of departments and their associated priorities will shift materially toward the graduate program and toward a structure more suited to some interdepartmental relations in graduate study and research.

West Coast Public University. West Coast Public University (WCPU), which opened in 1965, was planned with certain emphases: (1) A system of semiautonomous colleges is the basic unit for social, physical, and academic matters, and provides a focus for student and faculty identification. (2) Initially concentration is on undergraduate liberal education, with varying definitions and emphases in the various colleges. (3) A restricted curriculum is focused on the needs and interests of students rather than of the faculty. (4) Tutorials, seminars, and independent study are used extensively. (5) Early distinction has been sought in the arts and sciences. (6) Ultimate development of graduate and research programs will depend upon the peculiar opportunities afforded by the WCPU pattern.

The college design—architecturally, curricularly, and socially—is distinctive. The majority of students and some faculty members from each college live on campus and continuously interact in social and cultural programs. Each college is headed by a resident provost, assisted by resident preceptors. The fellows of the college, drawn from many fields, plan with the provost a program of courses for both lower and upper division. Some courses, unique to each college, are interdisciplinary and experimental in content and method. Provosts report directly to the president but also work closely with the three vice-presidents, who head the divisions of humanities, social sciences, and sciences.

Within the divisions, the boards of studies function as

the WCPU surrogate for traditional departments. Thus far, every faculty member has to be in some board of studies as well as a college. Salaries are paid 50 per cent by a college and 50 per cent by a division, although by rough estimate the faculty member teaches college-sponsored courses for only about 20 per cent of his teaching load.

Conflicts have arisen in the hiring and rewarding of faculty. For original appointments a board of studies, a college, and a vice-president must concur. The colleges seek individuals interested in teaching and in undergraduate students; the boards seek distinction in research and publication.

Promotions, salary increases, and terminations also present troublesome decisions, since a board of studies may be dissatisfied with the performance of an individual who has given highly meritorious service to one of the colleges. To complicate the matter further, the students may apply criteria different from those of other groups. Although the emphasis in the boards of studies (as in the university generally) is already heavy on research, graduate program expansion will increase the pressure for research and the amount of time needed for work with graduate students. An expressed hope is that some graduate work will be interdisciplinary and that graduate students, like the faculty, will be related to one of the colleges. This may happen to some extent in the humanities and social sciences, but it is not likely in the sciences.

Faculty load is unlike that found in most institutions. As members of boards of studies, faculty members are concerned with both undergraduate and graduate majors. In addition, if faculty members function as intended, they spend many hours in the college in contact with students and in team planning of college interdisciplinary courses. Student involvement complicates and slows down the deliberations. At the same time, the faculty member is always aware that the system of rewards through the boards of studies gives little weight to such service.

Originally, each college was to have some special view or interpretation of liberal education, and to some extent this remains true. But as new faculty and students develop their interests, these themes have been somewhat obscured. It was also originally expected that required courses in the colleges would approximate 50 per cent of the students' program, but in practice students have objected to such requirements, and the number of courses that students have in common varies greatly from college to college.

Costs are a matter of concern. Although university officials produce data to demonstrate that the operation is no more expensive per student than at other universities in the state (in fact, this was a requirement initially), there remains a prevalent suspicion that the costs are higher. In part, this is created by the charm of the campus and its buildings. But in great part, the suspicion has been generated by the fact that the university, in order to develop its several colleges, has had to raise money from private sources. Even if the costs to the state have not been more than at other state universities, it is still conceivable that the total cost per student is higher at WCPU. Is this competition with private universities justified? If indeed the costs (including capital expenditures) are actually higher, does the quality of education justify higher costs? These are questions that arouse deep emotion, but we found no adequate answers. As with the new universities in England, little evaluation has been made at WCPU of the impact of the educational program and the living experiences.

Trends for WCPU are not clear. Interviewees favorable to the college structure suggested that colleges rather than boards will define majors and B.A. general requirements, leaving boards to control only those courses used to satisfy the requirements. WCPU plans to construct buildings for social sciences and humanities, thereby predictably strengthening departmentalism. The sciences, both at WCPU and the newer English universities, have not readily accepted or accommodated themselves to a college pattern. Their laboratories provide an excuse; but the research emphasis and the accumulative nature of the disciplines, coupled with their relative abstractness, cause scientists to view the college pattern as almost irrelevant to their major concerns and aspirations. Another possibility—which is not widely discussed at WCPU, perhaps in deference to the president, whose vision and efforts made the major contribution to WCPU—is that the boards of studies will ultimately become budgeted departments and that the colleges will become minor satellites. Pressures in this direction are apparent. Some people see it as inevitable. The younger, untried faculty members feel more pressure under the WCPU pattern than do the established senior individuals, who originally were attracted to WCPU because of its innovative character and the unusual opportunity provided to explore their ideas about undergraduate education. A new president can hardly make his reputation on the basis of accepting the existing pattern; so a future president may not feel inclined to resist the pressures for reversion to a more traditional departmental organization. Weighing all factors, we do not see the college structure long maintaining its role as the predominant organizational feature.

New North Central University. The academic structure of New North Central University includes four colleges—Environmental Sciences, Human Biology, Creative Communication, and Community Sciences—and a School of Professional Studies. Each college includes several units called a "concentration," defined as "a group of faculty members with a common ecological problem orientation or interest." Each concentration has a chairman appointed by the dean and an executive committee of tenured members. Every faculty member belongs to a concentration.

Concentrations approve courses and define degree programs and majors (subject to further approval by one of the two divisional committees). The university's "Academic Plan" brochure states: "A student must select an environmental problem (or concentration) on which to focus. A concentration requires thirty credits at the junior-senior level reflecting an interdisciplinary focus on an environmental problem."

Although concentrations are "housed" within certain colleges, they function across college boundaries. For example, the Modernization Processes concentration considers problems relevant to all four colleges. Also, the faculty members of one concentration frequently teach in concentrations at other colleges. Concentrations exercise most of the functions usually assigned to departments; faculty members are hired, promoted, and generally cared for by their concentration.

Every faculty member also belongs to another academic unit called an "option," defined as "a group of faculty members . . . with a common or closely related disciplinary or professional interest." Originally, options were assigned to various colleges; but that system created confusion, since a faculty member's option could be in a college different from that of his concentration. In NNCU's first year, options tended to function as quasi-departments, even though the usual departmental functions were assigned to the concentration. The disciplines represented by the options apparently presented a more secure basis for faculty organization than did the newly defined concentrations.

A recent revision of the NNCU structure has replaced the college deans by a Dean of the Colleges. This new dean has four assistant deans, whose responsibilities are more university-wide than college-related. A new position of associate dean has been created to coordinate the options and the Liberal Education Seminars (the general education component of the NNCU plan). Options are now university-wide. Each concentration chairman now initiates his own budget request and controls his own budget, whereas formerly a college dean controlled the budget for an entire college. The Dean of the Colleges, however, determines concentrations' budget assignment and has operating funds of his own.

NNCU administrators believe these revisions will unify the collegiate structure, increase the authority and responsibility of the concentration chairmen, and separate the options more clearly from the operating and decision-making channels of the institution.

The new structure is expected to encourage both inter-college and intracollege communication by the concentrations. It also raises questions as to whether the colleges will—or should—continue; whether one inclusive collegiate unit or four colleges will best serve the university's objectives. One reason—perhaps minor—why the colleges may continue as at present is that the university's physical plans call for four structures grouped around a library, each structure serving a college. Another reason is that the theme college is meant to provide a "home" for both faculty and students.

Regression to departmentalism is an ever present possibility. The recruitment of new faculty based on the option's (discipline's) needs rather than on concentrations' or college needs would encourage departmentalization, so that faculty strongly committed to the interdisciplinary rather than departmental organization must be sought and appropriately rewarded.

An administrator who came to NNCU partly because of his dislike for the departmental boundaries at his former university expressed concern that the disciplines may assert themselves when the founding generation departs. This possibility is much in the minds of everyone at NNCU. Junior faculty are restive; the existing pattern constitutes a threat to mobility. Perhaps the most significant single question is whether any atypical organization and curricular structure devised by an administration for a new institution can long be defended against the specialized disciplinary interests of an expanding faculty. Only time can provide the answer to that question.

East Coast State University. When the East Coast State University was planned, it was intended to be an outstanding university in a state university system. Stars (widely known researchers, Nobel Prize winners) were sought for administrators and the initial faculty. Overnight ECSU acquired a reputation as an exciting and intellectual institution, possibly *the* research and graduate-level university of the state system. But its planners also sought to be innovative in undergraduate education, and here it seems that predictions went awry.

According to the original plan, ECSU proposed to create a residential college structure, each to enroll about sixty students. The model, as interpreted by some persons at ECSU, was the residence system at Harvard or Yale. In the original plan, courses related to the interests of residents would be offered in each college. However, since students were assigned to colleges by the housing bureau, such courses were difficult to plan. In addition, the residence halls, built under fund limitations, were not really suited for residential colleges. Actual college size has ranged from 200 to 450. Thus, the emphasis turned chiefly to the social and cultural aspects of student life, and the institution's major concern came to be that colleges should somehow serve as an antidote to impersonality. The role of the colleges never was defined clearly; several attempts to do so met with little success.

Masters of the colleges were to be selected from the faculty (from the departments) and were to give half time to leadership in the college, but masters were difficult to find because it was usually clear that their departmental futures would be jeopardized. Departments were already disenchanted by the size and quality of the undergraduate student load and were not always cooperative in releasing talent to the colleges.

Obviously, one problem was that the faculty was recruited in the expectation of establishing a strong graduate research university. The major concerns and the allocation of resources, therefore, were centered in the departments which were not really interested in innovative undergraduate education, doubted its necessity, despised its atypical interdisciplinary courses, and coveted the resources that might be diverted to it. And ECSU soon found that its resources were all too limited to accomplish its several goals.

It would be futile to attempt to assign blame. Administrators launching new institutions are faced with many and complex decisions; and as faculty, chairmen, and deans are selected, many of the original and fondest dreams are shattered by the emerging reality. This seems to be what happened at ECSU.

Western Private University. At Western Private University, the Arts and Science College (ASC), oldest unit in the institution, is undergoing an identity crisis. The problem is partly indicated in the matter of name. For its first fifty years the whole institution was called a college. Then, in the 1960s, the designation was changed to university, reflecting the development of a composite structure with several units including professional schools and cluster colleges. Another part of the identity crisis has resulted from the addition of cluster colleges, which compete with ASC for students, budget, and space.

ASC's identity crisis is expressed in the following alternatives. ASC could become one of several coequal colleges, stressing undergraduate education and basing its operations (such as faculty hiring and evaluation) upon a value system appropriate to its teaching function. Or ASC could remain the heart of the university, embracing all levels of instruction from freshman to Ph.D. as well as research in the disciplines. The first alternative is unacceptable, for ASC would then lose its identity. With the second, the cluster colleges would remain peripheral to ASC, competing with it and denying to its departments the services of specialists who could significantly ease the teaching burden and provide courses not now covered by the ASC staff. A third alternative, scarcely mentionable, would be elimination of the cluster colleges.

The cluster-college system, which began in 1962 with College A, has posed as many problems as it has solved. One purpose was to permit WPU to grow while retaining its close student-faculty relationships. It has retained that atmosphere (almost too much so for financial reasons), since the student-faculty ratio in the three cluster colleges is less than 10 to 1. But the colleges have not added many students to the university enrollment; in fall 1970, less than six hundred students were in cluster colleges.

The planning for these cluster colleges seems to have been inadequate. They were planned to have 250 students, but overhead and instructional costs are such that 600–700 students each would be sounder economically (according to one of the college provosts). Recruitment and retention of students and faculty has been more difficult than anticipated (although the experience varies from college to college). Good faculty apparently were discouraged by the lack of opportunity for long-range career development, especially the lack of graduate programs.

The intimate atmosphere in the colleges has backfired in some cases. Some faculty members find the intimacy claustrophobic (none now live in the college residence). For students, the intimacy sometimes created a family atmosphere that encouraged them to see the college *in loco parentis* and to develop a dependence on the faculty. The students seem both to want and to resent this dependence.

On the positive side, the college system introduced diversity into a traditional setting. A different breed of student, faculty, and program came to WPU with College A and its sister colleges. The colleges also introduced the idea of an orderly process of growth through a form of federation. Departments have visualized the possibility of building new or better programs if the several college faculties could be more extensively shared.

In many basic matters, the cluster colleges have had very little actual effect on ASC. College A's atypical calendar made any relationship almost impossible, and it has functioned almost entirely separate from ASC. College B's geographical-area emphasis and bilingual emphasis have also limited its possible relations with ASC. The clearest effect of cluster colleges upon ASC seems to have been the ASC faculty's resentment, caused by their belief that College A was being improperly favored in office space, contact hours, class size, and money. The favoritism issue was aggravated by what ASC regards as elitist attitudes in College A. At present, ASC's anticollege resentment focuses on the expense of the cluster colleges, and this resentment is heightened by a second issue stemming from disciplinary interests—for example, a conflict over efforts to develop an anthropology concentration in College C, which threatened efforts to add new resources to ASC.

Clearly, the cluster colleges, created to solve problems of undergraduate education, precipitated a questioning of the entire university structure. Their future would have been uncertain for the many reasons mentioned here, but the president who fostered them originally is now deceased. With new leadership, budgetary crises, and a dubious record of success for the cluster colleges, the future is unpredictable.

Eastern State University. Eastern State University, for many years a private institution, became a campus of the state university system in 1962. In 1966, a new president arrived and began a period of reorganization. That period entered a new phase in the spring of 1970, following the president's resignation (to assume a more prestigious presidency) and a near disastrous student-faculty-community conflict.

The reorganization aimed to "change the tone at ESU . . . to change the set of expectations" of people on and off campus. It sought to create a new sense of community and to increase relationships and communication within the university. The organization was not explicitly proposed to reduce departmental autonomy, but it was expected to do exactly that. New structures were created, each intended to serve a distinctive purpose: (1) central administration, a staff of vice-presidents and advisors—intended to decentralize the administration; (2) Faculties,[1] seven groups of departments and schools, each headed by a provost—intended to overcome departmental separatism, allow increased interdisciplinary work, and provide a framework for interrelating academic and professional concerns within the broad intellectual fields; (3) a senate composed of all faculty, including all administrators holding faculty appointment—a "town meeting," chaired by the president and guided by an executive committee; (4) university-wide deanships (or instructional divisions), one each for undergraduate, graduate, and adult continuing education—intended to serve the needs of students and faculty at the various educational levels; (5) colleges, chiefly residential units which would provide a "home" and focus of identification for all students— expressing the "personality" and interests of their members through cocurricular social and cultural activities.

During 1969–70, the administration of ESU included the following positions: one president, eight vice-presidents, seven presidential advisors and assistants, four associate and assistant vice-presidents, ten directors, seven provosts (of Faculties), one associate provost, three deans (university-wide), ten deans (within Faculties), five masters (of colleges), one ombudsman, one advocate, one dean (of a council), one chairman (of a select

---

[1] "Faculties" with a capital *F* refers to the structural units; "faculties" with a small *f* refers to the instructional personnel.

committee), and eighty-one chairmen of academic departments.

This top-heavy administration (so it was widely regarded on the campus) undoubtedly was introduced, at least in part, because of the prediction that the campus would increase greatly, perhaps doubling in enrollment during the 1970s. The faculty would, of course, grow proportionately to the student body, depending on the student-faculty ratio adopted. Also, the campus was intended to grow physically through the addition of a new 1,200-acre site some miles distant. This expansion would also require an increased administrative staff. For several complex reasons (chiefly political), the new campus was not begun on schedule, although money had been appropriated by the state. The expansion of enrollment and support of research also slacked off.

Powers and responsibilities of the several positions were unclear. For example, a provost told us that for some problems he was never sure which of two administrators he should consult. He solved his dilemma by sending two memos to cover each problem: one memo with one name listed first and circled, and the other listed second; then another memo with the order of names reversed. No carbon copies, only originals. The administrators would then get together—supposedly each one believing himself the key figure—and determine the issue on an ad hoc basis.

Seven Faculties were established, each headed by a provost controlling the budget and the hiring-promoting procedures. However, the provost's actual power was perceived by most of our interviewees as considerably less than his position's formal power. Departments are at least as autonomous as they were before the reorganization and in some cases more so. Two aspects of the reorganization were important for preserving or enlarging departmental autonomy: first, the general confusion and ambiguity in the administrative structure; and second, the value system of the "expert university" which the new administration encouraged. The chairmen had been accustomed to presenting their requests and recommendations to a dean and a faculty policy committee in each of the academic units. So, when the provosts replaced the deans, the effect on the chairmen was insignificant. But the appointment of university-wide deans (graduate school, university college, adult education college) added another voice to the proceedings and diluted the provosts' authority, for the deans could strengthen the chairmen vis-à-vis the provosts by endorsing departmental programs that were not high on the provosts' priority list.

The second dysfunctional aspect of the reorganization concerns the basic consideration (the values) involved in reorganizing the university. The president wanted to make ESU the equal of the University of California at Berkeley, Harvard, and other top-rated universities. So ESU adopted the values and criteria of the "great" mid-twentieth-century American universities and sought to achieve excellence by means of research-oriented, publish-or-perish, discipline-oriented faculties. An ESU faculty member commented: "The concept of the 'expert university' means having within it people who are acknowledged experts in given fields . . . career-oriented . . . organizational buccaneers . . . cosmopolitans, who really don't have a commitment to [the university] . . . each tries to build his own turf . . . the structure is an extremely competitive one." This value system gives prestige to departments that operate in accordance with it. Thus, the provosts were at a disadvantage when their priorities contradicted those of chairmen who could exhibit their "stars" in self-defense. Changing the university structure by setting up Faculties was not likely to affect the university's operations so long as departmental values prevailed.

The proposed colleges were defined as follows:

[They will be] centers of identification for students . . . nondegree granting . . . headed by a master . . . will aid the general education program . . . by assisting with advisement and by offering experimental courses through appropriate faculty bodies.

We propose that all students . . . have the opportunity to associate with or live in a college which will include residential and dining facilities . . . as well as cultural facilities.

Each of the colleges may be expected to develop a character of its own. . . . No more than a thousand students . . .

although the sizes of the colleges would vary. Similarly, the
mix of . . . students would vary.

Proposals for the colleges were discussed during 1968–69.
In fall 1969, fifteen units began operations: five colleges and
ten workshops conceived as proto-colleges. During 1969–70 discussion of the best organization and the proper role for the colleges continued.

In spring 1970 the faculty senate adopted a new plan for
the collegiate system, giving the colleges autonomy equal to
that of the University College and the Faculties, with budget-
initiating authority, its own policy-making assembly, and a director appointed by the president with the assembly's advice
and consent. Each college is expected to have markedly more
self-direction under this plan. Increased ability to respond to
changing conditions—by relatively informal modes of creation
and dissolution—may ultimately keep the system relevant,
meaningful, and effective, although whether any higher education unit will precipitate its own dissolution remains to be seen.
Greater variety among colleges is expected to result from this
increased flexibility.

One of the proposals in the original reorganization was
to expand the University College from a two-year to a four-year
unit. The proposal called for a school of undergraduate and
general studies to ensure that each student receiving his first
degree will be an educated man. UC has no teaching staff of
its own, but all faculty members who teach undergraduates are
automatically members of UC and eligible to attend its meetings. This group recommends for admission and degree requirements to the faculty senate. Several standing and ad hoc
committees consider UC problems, but the University College
has no formal means of effecting its objectives. The situation was
stated succinctly by the UC dean in his Annual Report, 1968–
69: "University College must rely upon influence rather than
power, persuasion rather than command, coordination rather
than coercion. There is a strange paradox here. The extraordi-
nary responsibilities of University College . . . are not backed
up by the means of control standard to institutions of higher

education. University College has at this point relatively little say in such critical issues as faculty appointment, retention, and promotion, although coordination in these areas would seem appropriate, in the abstract." UC also lacked the resources for freshman seminars, experimental courses, independent study, and remedial study, which were expected to be features of its programs. The task of improving undergraduate education without either auxiliary staff or funds is essentially impossible.

Evaluation of the reorganization at ESU varies with individuals. Some view the events as chaos created by a theorist (the former president) who wished to achieve several conflicting goals, but who was also so involved in external affairs that he was unaware of or insensitive to the paralysis and confusion created by the changes. Because of this confusion, changes aimed at wresting control of undergraduate education from the departments permitted them to emerge with increased stature and autonomy.

There have been numerous changes in personnel at ESU. Indeed, an era has been concluded and a new one begun. With a new administration everything becomes uncertain again.

OTHER PATTERNS OF REORGANIZATION

There are many other patterns of organization and reorganization than those in this chapter. For example, reorganization of the college of arts and sciences on a large university campus is quite common. The sheer size of a college that includes the arts, social sciences, humanities, and natural sciences presents a major problem of coordination and control. In some universities, associate deans or directors have been assigned to coordinate the activities of groups of departments. But the typical experience has been that these individuals are ineffective if they do not have an input to budgetary allocations; on the other hand, if they do determine the budgets of those units assigned to them, then de facto the college has been broken up into separate units. The most common pattern breaks the arts and science college into three or four colleges, with such groupings as fine arts, humanities, social science, and natural science. Alternatively, the fine arts may be part of the humanities, or the natural sciences may be broken into biological and the physical sciences.

Wenger (1971) reports on a visit to nine universities, six of which have changed from a single college to several disciplinary colleges. According to Wenger, the large colleges, in addition to their administrative problems, generate an impersonality that alienates students and to some extent the faculty. Productive discussions of undergraduate education are impossible, and little innovation in undergraduate education comes from such large colleges. Evidence for this is found in the extent to which residential colleges, cluster colleges, and other variations of liberal-arts colleges have been introduced into the university. The major reasons for breaking the single college into a number of disciplinary colleges are, in part, educational: smaller size, greater homogeneity in students and faculty, and innovation in instruction and curriculum.

Accountability is also a factor. In a large university, with departments representing all disciplines, no one dean is adequately familiar with all the departments in his particular school or college. Hence, the departments acquire a high degree of autonomy and demonstrate a low level of accountability. With smaller, more homogeneous units, a dean can have more insight into the departments and exert more leadership. The total administrative costs increase with the number of units involved; however, the additional costs of administration may be overbalanced by more efficient use of resources by smaller units.

> The additional administrative energy made available by the appointment of deans over smaller and more homogeneous collections of departments can increase the fiscal accountability of these units; permit the better planning and setting of priorities for the disciplines within the college; and provide additional time for educational leadership. On the other hand, efforts to preserve the unity and integrity of liberal education and to generate interdisciplinary activity by appointing a dean (without line authority) to coordinate among the disciplinary colleges and their deans have met with little success at those institutions visited which have had time to try it [Wenger, 1971, p. 2].

Wenger's "dean (without line authority)" refers to attempts by universities to insert into the administrative structure
coordinative roles unsupported by budget control. Wenger's
observation that such deans are ineffective parallels similar observations in this study. (See Eastern State University, p. 74ff.)

Those who bemoan the loss of unity in liberal education
when the arts and sciences are divided have a point in theory.
But in practice the various units of the arts and sciences in a
large university are so committed to research and graduate
work, so professionalized, and so little aware of the needs of
undergraduate students that distress about loss of unity seems
misplaced.

Disciplinary colleges are less likely to insist upon distribution requirements which include courses offered in other
colleges. Experiences in the English universities confirm this.
Perhaps such colleges are correct since it may be unrealistic in
the present day to insist that students specializing in social
sciences or humanities be required to enroll in the natural
sciences. Moreover, by attaining homogeneity of student body
and faculty the organization into disciplinary colleges makes
more sense than does the unusual college pattern reported for
South Coastal State University (pp. 61ff).

How much the disciplinary colleges can restore personal
attention is dubious in a large university. These colleges may
themselves be so large that their impact in that direction is
negligible. Breaking down the arts and science departments into
smaller groups does not change the faculty's value system. If
they were primarily interested in research and graduate education, they will continue to be so. Interdisciplinary courses cutting across humanities, social sciences, and the natural sciences
become more difficult when college boundaries intervene, but
the incidence of such courses is rare in any case, and some
special vehicle for interdisciplinary courses is required in the
university.

Departments find in the smaller colleges that the dean is
more aware of their activities and more likely to understand
them. Departmental autonomy may be reduced thereby. The
department may have to work harder to support marginal activities which, in a larger unit, would have been unknown to the

dean. If resources are scarce and departments do not automatically get more funds because of an increased production of
credit hours, the smaller disciplinary colleges may lose interest
in the service aspect of their instructional program. Such indifference or recalcitrance may be more difficult to resolve in a
system with autonomous colleges and several deans than in a
single college.

The natural sciences are more professional in their orientation and generally more favorable toward separate disciplinary-based colleges than are the humanities and social sciences.
However, the arts, humanities, and the social sciences may
gain by the separation, since their budgets are thereby somewhat screened from the laboratory expenses of the natural
sciences.

It is questionable whether undergraduate education is
improved by splitting a college of arts and sciences into a number of units. If faculty members play a decisive role in choice
of a dean, they will pick a person who has made his mark by
research and involvement in graduate education. As dean, he
may become—as most deans seem to—more interested in undergraduate education, but find that his efforts are frustrated by
faculty expectations and his obligation to meet them. Really
competent deans are hard to find. If one good dean is hard to
find, the search for three or four is certainly no easier. As more
than one university has found, ineffective administration of a
large unit is simply replaced by ineffective administration of
three or four smaller ones. Central administrators—instead of
confronting a single dean of a large conglomerate, whose various interests he cannot adequately represent—may confront a
series of deans, each strongly and persistently representing the
interests of his constituents.

Some universities are establishing units that are neither
colleges nor departments but have some characteristics of both.
In one university we visited, the Institute of Technology includes two distinctive overlapping units: professional engineering departments and engineering science research centers. The
departments have responsibility for degree programs, curriculum design, and enforcement of academic standards; the centers

have responsibility for laboratories, academic courses, and research programs. The problems of a rapidly changing technology are serious for engineering schools. New fields of specialization are continually emerging, often creating new patterns of relationship such as engineering science, engineering physics, nuclear physics, and computer sciences. The systems concept is both highly specialized and broad in its implication. The traditional departmental organization of civil, mechanical, electrical, chemical, and other such specializations has still some meaning in various industries and has some sanction in terms of the existence of professional societies by those names. But there is a need, as exemplified by the plan just mentioned, to develop another approach to the undergraduate program in engineering. Rosenstein and Cromwell (1968) have suggested programs built around basic work and design with "stems" of material, energy, information, and general education—topped off by integrative programs related to systems. A number of universities have already moved in this direction.

The problem in engineering is symptomatic of the problem throughout the university. The disciplines exist and have some sanction. They are no longer the best vehicle for providing instruction either at the graduate or undergraduate level, and they are also unsatisfactory for sponsoring research oriented to problems outside of the university. As yet, however, no generally acceptable alternative exists.

PROBLEMS CREATED BY ORGANIZATIONAL PATTERNS

Organizational innovations have been designed to solve various problems, including neglect of undergraduate education, lack of accountability, indifference to social problems, inadequate interdisciplinary programs, overspecialized research, lack of faculty identification with the institution, and generally the intractability of departments in modifying their ways or changing their priorities to meet changing demands and needs. Our examples give ample evidence that these problems may not be solved—and, indeed, may be exacerbated—or may take an unanticipated twist. The new organizational patterns may in themselves create problems. In the new English universities, the school and college patterns reflect a direct attack on some of the problems of undergraduate education. Departments have been accused of duplication of efforts, but the school structure, if anything, increases this possibility. However, when one is committed, as in the English universities, to a rather expensive pattern of education involving a faculty-student ratio which is high by United States standards, duplication may not be a concern. In each of the new English universities, whether departments formally exist or not, subject groups are organized and play an increasingly significant role in the university.

Communication problems have eased between students and faculty and also between smaller groups of faculty within a particular school or college, but the members of subject groups have difficulty communicating with each other or developing a continuing program of course planning and research. Faculty members associated with more than one school find in Britain, as here, that keeping up contacts in two areas usurps a very large proportion of one's time. Confusions of authority also arise. As the universities grow, communication will certainly become more complicated. Schools that were once relatively small, no larger than many of our departments, are increasing in size, and informal approaches are becoming less effective.

In the newer English universities, the founding fathers and the early appointees were enchanted by an opportunity to carry out activities that they had long thought desirable, while newer faculty members coming into the university do not fully understand the existing pattern of organization and tend to revert to disciplinary specialization and push in that direction.

This tendency is reinforced by the fact that graduate programs—which, in these new universities, developed side by side with the baccalaureate programs—have been largely based on traditional disciplines. New faculty members joining the universities after the first few years find the graduate program more appropriate to their interests and more akin to a traditional departmental organization. This, in turn, creates undercurrents of dissatisfaction with the baccalaureate honors degree programs, which in the more traditional universities are highly specialized.

Taking all factors into account, a reasonable hypothesis is that within five or six years all of these English universities will be departmentalized in fact if not in name. Some deans and faculty say they are now. It is also reasonable to predict that, even with departmentalization, degree programs will retain a broader base than the traditional, single-discipline honors degree. Enough students and faculty find values in the flexibility provided in deciding on a major and in the need for broader training for many jobs to assure continuance of the pattern.

Our case studies of United States institutions indicate somewhat similar problems. There are indications that, as patterns become fixed, early enthusiasm wanes. The faculty members who gladly spent many hours during the early stages feel the need to relax a bit. The forces of renovation may then turn to the reinstitution of a traditional pattern.

A large percentage of the departmental faculty in most universities is really composed of second-class citizens in the sense that they are not widely known researchers or scholars. Nevertheless, any new unit devoted to undergraduate education raises the bugaboo of second-class citizenship. So long as an individual must keep his foot in two or more units (department, board of studies, disciplinary group, school, college) and so long as in one of them research and scholarly activity become a prime condition for salary increase and promotion, the individual in several camps faces an unreasonably heavy load in teaching, student contacts, committee work, and general anxiety and mental strain. He still is expected to engage in scholarly work. The one who minimizes his contribution to the school or college and concentrates on his specialization, research, and graduate students will get ahead and seldom hear more than a mild criticism that he contributes little to the undergraduate program. The individual who becomes so engrossed with the undergraduate program that he loses sight of departmental priorities is due for some anxious moments, and he creates some troublesome moments for others. Yet, in the main, our case studies demonstrate that many faculty members are required to keep a foot in two or more camps. Michigan State University has long had an undergraduate university college with its own departments employing their own staff, but this is atypical. Full-time undergraduate teachers will always risk designation as second-class citizens, but one who finds promotions and salary increments coming on schedule on the basis of his instructional activity can afford to ignore that designation.

Many new programs raise problems of communication because of their complexity. When a university maintains an existing department and college structure and then tries to weave through this another coordinating structure, the resulting pattern creates a situation in which nobody knows who is really responsible. (See Eastern State University, pp. 72ff.) Also, in such patterns duplication of effort may be tremendous. Many people have to view the same things from different viewpoints. A professor walking out of a college committee discussion of a particular problem may walk right into another discussion of the same problem in a department, board of studies, or university-level committee. Colleges initiated to provide an innovative brand of education may find that as students and faculty change, the innovations grow irrelevant. In some cases, as at Western Private University, new colleges have frozen into a pattern in which students and faculty reject modifications even when enrollment drops. With experimental programs, the first year seems the best. Thereafter, things become fixed, and the incoming students and faculty find themselves prisoners of a structure which they do not grasp and which they did not create.

A number of reorganizations have assigned individuals responsibilities without sufficient authority. The college provost who needs a board of studies' approval for hiring or rewarding his faculty finds it difficult to assemble a corps of people whose primary concern is the college. The provost finds much of his time devoted to resolving difficult situations created by dual roles of staff, so that his leadership role in the college itself suffers. An individual who is asked to head any new program should insist that he be permitted to appoint some staff who are fully responsible to him and also that he be given a piece of the budgets that affect people who are only partly responsible to him.

None of these new programs has been able to avoid a departmental type of operating unit in some form. Both students and faculty demand a recognized designation as a sociologist or a sociology major, and so on. In the new universities, students wonder whether they have had enough work in a discipline to make their degree a sound one. At New North Central University, students insisted on a structure in which they could identify with a particular discipline, with graduate or professional school admissions prominent in their thinking.

The graduate school may be the critical factor. Although some universities have attempted to introduce broad-based graduate degree programs, the general tendency in all institutions—new or reorganized—is to maintain, at the graduate level, the departmental structure and the highly specialized approach to the Ph.D. The graduate program both requires and sustains the departmental structure. But the departmental structure also impedes undergraduate programs based on nondepartmental or interdisciplinary approaches. So the person responsible for an undergraduate college or school undertakes a job for which the only available tools were developed for a different task.

Costs are always a problem. Despite discussions of more economical ways of conducting undergraduate education, most innovations move to a larger faculty-to-student ratio than is typical at the undergraduate level. Planners try to justify the costs by citing the value of the *forms* of education—expensive ones such as small classes, seminars, independent study—rather than citing any real improvement in the *quality* of education. West Coast Public University strongly resists comments on the fact that its undergraduate program is more expensive than elsewhere, although it has had to seek large sums of money from private sources in addition to state funding. The question must be raised whether publicly supported institutions should carry on expensive undergraduate programs of unknown merit simply because some administrators, faculty, or students like it that way.

Another problem is the general unwillingness of innovators to examine themselves critically. The development of new programs is arduous and time-consuming, a task which has many critics. Those directly involved are risking their professional careers. They do not want—or cannot afford—any critical evidence that could be used against them; demands for evaluation or the offer of a critical evaluation may generate severe emotional reactions, as we found in instances during our campus visits. Those operating in ambivalent, undefined, and unsupported roles can be driven to depths of frustration. The contradictions between the dream and the reality, readily apparent to the unbiased observer, are difficult to perceive or to admit by those imbedded in these programs.

CONCLUSIONS

Frustrations obviously exist in traditional departmentalized programs, or else new organizations and curricular patterns would not be sought. But new patterns may generate other frustrations or perhaps rearrange the old ones. Some of those we have encountered are the following:

Faculty. New programs involving multiple roles add greatly to the faculty's load—more committees, more student contacts, time-consuming course and curricular development, and continuing pressures for research.

Tensions are produced by multiple assessments; no one person evaluates the totality of faculty effort.

An identity crisis is created by nondepartmental organizations and programs: they do not coincide with labels used by professional societies, they may hinder faculty mobility between institutions, and they may create a second-class faculty on a campus.

Curriculum. The uncertainties of nondisciplinary curricular development raise questions about academic standards and about overlapping or duplication in courses and programs.

Mere conjunction of courses from several disciplines— no matter how innovative—does not produce integration.

Interdisciplinary course development and teaching are arduous and continuous. Such courses never really settle down, and should not.

Innovative curriculums frequently result only in new compartmentalizations. One rigidity is exchanged for another.

Authority, Administration, and Management. Communication is a serious problem throughout higher education, but new patterns of organization designed to alleviate it may actually aggravate it because an unfamiliar structure heightens sensitivities and insecurities.

Atypical organizations are not easily geared into larger systems based on more traditional patterns.

Students. Students may find somewhat increased program flexibility in nondepartmentalized programs, but only if their interests coincide with the new boundary lines.

New programs (in the United States) have tended to attract students dissatisfied with the system, disenchanted with requirements and restrictions, and generally insistent on an equal voice among faculty and administration. Some of these students have serious academic interests; some do not. But anti-establishment attitudes by themselves do not necessarily produce good students or viable institutions.

Despite administrative and faculty predilections toward combination of living and learning in residence halls, students quite generally display antagonism toward residence halls and the demanding programs of residential colleges.

Other Issues. Many new programs appear to be more expensive than traditional ones because of increases in administrative personnel and larger faculty-to-student ratios. Facilities may also be more expensive, and it is not certain that this is compensated by dual-purpose usage.

Departmental autonomy is generally decreased by innovative structures, but problems of autonomy—excess or deficient—are merely shifted to other points in the structure. Furthermore, no structure observed has been able to curb or satisfy the faculty's desires for a disciplinary-based structure corresponding to their graduate school preparation and their research interests.

5

Collective Bargaining: Freedom Versus Equality

General economic conditions of the early 1970s contributed to the growth of collective bargaining in higher education. Well-trained and highly qualified specialists were faced with unemployment. Faculty members in some universities found that tenure did not mean security from economic downturn and that colleagues in unionized faculties maintained job security as well as attaining higher salaries. Some faculty members who had been accustomed to transferring to grant or contract accounts also found those funds drying up. Faculty members began to question the extent of their job security, their mobility, and their estimate of education as a growth industry. Higher education has faced temporary setbacks in the past, and many faculty members still feel no necessity for changing their way of life. They still feel confident that legislatures and governing boards will not terminate faculty because of economic conditions—as is permissible under the rules of tenure. But uncertainty and frustrations are apparent on many university campuses; and many faculty members, noting the success of collective bargaining elsewhere, are attracted to this approach. Collective bargaining may be the wave of the near future, and its implications for institutional autonomy require consideration.

Collective bargaining in higher education might pit student and junior faculty demands for equality against those senior faculty members and administrators who cherish their personal freedom. (The split between non-tenure and tenure-track faculty is so strong at City University of New York that each has its own bargaining unit.) Unions raise the banner of equality; students and junior faculty march along; tenured faculty and administrators rally round freedom's flag; and the battle is joined. In *Lessons of History* (1968), the Durants identify this conflict as a major theme of history: "Freedom and equality are sworn and everlasting enemies, and when one prevails the other dies. . . . only the man who is below average in economic ability desires equality; those who are conscious of superior ability desire freedom." In higher education the conflict is likely to intensify unless the "haves" begin to share their decision-making powers, or an external agent renders the "haves" into "have nots." (A five-year review of tenure, abolition of tenure, or mandatory salary reduction for faculty members over sixty could have this effect.)

The growth rate of material written on collective bargaining in higher education probably now exceeds the rate at which institutions are adopting collective bargaining. Literature on the subject has now expanded into both popular journals (*Harper's,* October 1971) and scholarly journals (*Wisconsin Law Review,* 1971). *The Chronicle of Higher Education* has few issues that do not include a recent report on court, university, and union activities associated with collective bargaining. The eventual growth of collective bargaining can only be guessed.

One must remember that it took only nine years to organize 65 per cent of the nation's school teachers for collective bargaining. Two teacher unions, The National Education As-

sociation (1,000,000 members) and the American Federation of
Teachers (250,000 members), achieved this result in fierce competition with each other for teacher members. Both the NEA
and the AFT (including their state and local affiliates) have
made impressive gains in salaries, fringe benefits, and working
conditions by hard bargaining and willingness to take other
militant job actions. It is virtually certain that college and
university faculty will follow this pattern in the 1970s [Lieber-
man, 1971, p. 62].

Israel Kugler, president of the American Federation of
Teachers, estimates that all university faculty will be organized
by the end of this decade.

HISTORICAL ASPECTS

The trade-union movement in this country began prior
to the Civil War, but with economic fluctuations and the lack
of supporting legislation unions were unstable and often dis-
appeared during periods of economic downturn. The turn of
the century saw an increasing strength and stability of unions,
together with the introduction of collective bargaining as the
decision-making model. Pressures for collective bargaining came
primarily from management rather than from unions. Prior to
this development, union demands were unilateral; and if these
demands were not met immediately, strikes resulted. In the first
three decades of the twentieth century the Supreme Court dealt
with matters of boycotts, strikes, and other forms of union
coercion. In 1935, Congress passed the National Labor Relations Act, which had little effect until held constitutional by
the Supreme Court in 1937.

Since July 1970 most private universities have been subject to the jurisdiction of the National Labor Relations Board
(NLRB) and thus subject to federal jurisdiction and statutory
control. All public institutions of higher education, because of
a specific exemption in the National Labor Relations Act, are
subject to the jurisdiction of the individual states. Table 6
indicates states that have specific collective-bargaining laws.

One of the most important aspects of the NLRA is the
requirement that management must bargain exclusively with

an agent selected by its employees. Prior to this act negotiations between management and employees were generally conducted with an employee organization, whose membership was determined on a representational basis. The failure of this type of representational decision making has some implications for using a faculty senate as a bargaining unit (Livingston, 1969).

A second important provision of the NLRA is that the act specifically excludes supervisors from membership in a bargaining unit and provides that the designation of a supervisor may be strictly construed. The role of the department chairman is usually as ambiguous in collective bargaining as in the organizational structure of the university itself. Reviewing the case of Fordham University, the National Labor Relations Board held in September 1971 that department chairmen may be included in the faculty unit (Jacobson, 1971). In the past department chairmen and deans were considered supervisors and therefore ineligible to belong to the faculty collective-bargaining unit. Fordham had argued that all faculty members are actually supervisors along with chairmen because they take part in decisions on hiring, tenure, promotion, and matters of academic policy. In the same vein, the NLRB held that the "faculty exercises its role in policy determination only as a group" (Jacobson, 1971) which includes the chairmen. The traditional decision-making policy and practices at each university will probably determine the composition of the collective-bargaining unit.

Another interesting point was made in the Fordham decision. The NLRB held that any identifiable group of employees with a special community of interest may form its own bargaining unit separate from the university bargaining unit. This provision may make some sense for a professional school; but if it holds for a department or college, the resulting chaos would be hard to imagine.

ACADEMIC DILEMMA: PROFESSION OR VOCATION?

Several writers have suggested reasons why faculty members turn to collective bargaining. Lieberman (1971) notes that faculty members feel a need for protection against capricious

TABLE 6. SUMMARY OF COLLECTIVE-BARGAINING REGULATIONS AFFECTING INSTITUTIONS OF HIGHER EDUCATION

State	Year Enacted	Representation	Administration by	Negotiation-Impasse Procedures	Strike Provisions	Set Timetable
California	1968	Proportional	Public school employer to adopt reasonable rules and regulations	No specific provisions.	No specific provisions	None
Hawaii	1970	Exclusive	Hawaii Public Employment Relations Board	Procedures may culminate in final binding arbitration by mutual agreement.	Legal under conditions	Yes
Kansas	1970	Exclusive	State Board of Education	No specific provisions.	Prohibited	Yes
Maine	1969	Exclusive	Commissioner of Labor & Industry; Public Employees Labor Relations Appeal Board	Mediation and/or fact finding by mutual consent. Binding arbitration by agreement on salaries, pensions, insurance.	Prohibited	Yes
Massachusetts	1968	Exclusive	Board of Conciliation & Arbitration; Labor Relations Council	Fact finding with nonbinding recommendations.	Prohibited	Yes
Michigan	1965	Exclusive	Labor Mediation Board	Mediation & fact finding. Nonbinding recommendations via Labor Management Board.	Prohibited	None
Nebraska	1969	No specific provisions	School Board & State Court of Industrial Relations	Fact-finding & advisory recommendations.	No specific provisions	None
Nevada	1969	Exclusive	Local Government Employee Management Relations Board	Mediation via Local Government Employee-Management Relations Board after 45 days, fact finding after 75 days.	Prohibited	Yes

TABLE 6. SUMMARY OF COLLECTIVE-BARGAINING REGULATIONS AFFECTING INSTITUTIONS OF HIGHER EDUCATION—CONTINUED

State	Year Enacted	Representation	Administration by	Negotiation-Impasse Procedures	Strike Provisions	Set Time-table
New Jersey	1968	Exclusive	Public Employment Relations Commission	Mediation and fact finding with nonbinding recommendations via Public Employment Relations Commission.	No specific provisions	None
New York	1967	No specific provisions	Public Employment Relations Board	Parties to develop own procedures, may include binding arbitration. Mediation and fact finding available.	Prohibited	Yes
Pennsylvania	1970	Exclusive	Pennsylvania Labor Relations	Mutual voluntary binding arbitration permitted. Mediation & fact finding mandatory according to fixed "budget submission date" timetable.	Permitted with restrictions	Yes
South Dakota	1969	Formal or informal	Labor Commissioner (for unit structure and recognition only)	Mutually agree to a procedure or either party may request intervention by Commissioner of Labor.	Prohibited	None
Wisconsin	1967	Exclusive	Wisconsin Employment Relations Commission	Mediation: fact finding with nonbinding recommendations via Wisconsin Employee Relations Board.	Prohibited	None

Adapted from "Summary of State Collective-Bargaining Statutes Affecting Teachers," *Compact*, V (February 1971), 17-24.

93

or unfair management; weakness of faculty councils; and budgeting pressure upon basic salaries, tenure, sabbaticals, and
travel. Others mention the failure of historical administrative
patterns to adjust to growth and change; growing concern over
priorities in the assignment of ever decreasing resources; growing external control over institutional decision making; increasing production of Ph.D.s and a decreasing job market; and
decreasing faculty mobility due to general economic conditions.
The three classic union issues are wages, hours, and working
conditions, and closely related subissues include benefits, job
security, merit systems, definition of a bargaining unit, selection
of representatives, and grievances.

Unions usually prefer to negotiate in quantified terms.
A twelve-hour teaching load is as typical of union negotiations
as it is antithetical to academic traditions. Unions prefer to
bargain from fixed positions; many professors resent specificity,
which they feel limits their freedom. Therefore, some adjustments in attitudes must be made before faculty members and
union representatives can agree upon goals for wages and hours.

The vocational self-image of faculty members differs
from that of most union members. Faculty members—at least
up to now—have not felt that they are employees of the university, but rather that they *are* the university. They do not earn
wages paid "for work or services, as by the hour, day, or week";
instead, they earn a salary "periodically paid to a person for
regular work or services, especially work other than that of a
manual, mechanical, or menial kind." The publicly employed
college professor usually feels no occupational kinship with
plumbers or electricians. It is in labor's attractive total-compen-
sation package that professors find common interest.

Issues of academic wages and hours are difficult to identify in the standard trade-union terms, and strikes are in many
cases illegal (Sands, 1971). "Working conditions" is a term
more acceptable to faculty members than "wages" or "hours,"
but they already have a greater voice in their conditions of
employment than most trade unions would even suggest. Thus,
only after the classic issues of wages, hours, and working conditions have been modified do they have relevance to faculty

members. Otherwise, negotiations on "working conditions" could cost faculty members freedom to define their role as salaried professionals who do not work for an hourly wage and who already determine many employment conditions.

The subissues of benefits, job security, and merit systems do have meaning for faculty members. Fringe benefits—including insurance, retirement, medical and hospital plans—are already a part of most academic contracts. Additional sabbaticals, free tuition, and housing allowances are not uncommon, particularly at private institutions. Other benefits can be easily identified and added. For example, The American Federation of Teachers at the University of Florida stated in a promotional piece, *AFT Action in the University: A Dedicated Few Make a Majority:* " (1) The university shall provide funds such that each faculty member can attend two professional meetings per year. (2) Each tenured faculty member has the right to sabbatical leave. . . . In any one year, 5 per cent of the tenured faculty may be granted sabbatical leave. (3) The tuition for the family of faculty attending any state college or university in Florida shall be waived. (4) The university shall provide funds to establish a day-care center for the young children of faculty members." This list illustrates two points. First, possible fringe benefits have no limit. Competition to represent faculty runs high, and promises of benefits can easily be escalated. Second, the university administrators might be happy to support such proposals, but legislators control the required money. To state a proposed benefit more accurately one would have to say: "(4) The people of the State of Florida shall provide funds to establish a day-care center." In Florida at least, this would raise the same issue for all public employees. Competing unions may play their pipes, but legislatures eventually call the tune.

TENURE VS. CONTRACT

Job security is not identical with tenure and should be separated in collective-bargaining discussions. Many faculty members do not have tenure, and those who do may still lose it if their jobs are abolished through reorganization. Faculty resistance to change, especially when reorganizations are under discussion, is based in part upon their lack of job security. A continuing contract, as well as more formal procedures for granting and terminating employment, is certain to follow the decision to bargain collectively. The "up or out" policy at many universities may give way to formal hearings and grievance procedures specified in the contract.

Attacks upon tenure from within higher education seem to be growing. During recent hearings before the AAUP concerning the censure of four colleges for violation of academic freedom, one chairman is quoted as saying, "The AAUP's 1940 Statement of Principles on academic freedom and tenure today has as little relevance to modern-day college as the Dred Scott decision has to desegregation. It will be searched in vain for a declaration as to the college professor's responsibilities and obligations to the college he serves and the students he teaches." During the same proceedings, Bertram H. Davis, general secretary of the AAUP, acknowledged that administrators are "increasingly questioning" AAUP reports, which provide the bases for recommendations of censure. If the attacks on tenure continue to grow, inevitably faculty members will seek new methods and possibly new organizations with which to ensure academic freedom and personal security. Almost since the beginning of American unionism, collective-bargaining agreements have included an elaborate and well-defined grievance procedure to ensure against arbitrary and capricious discharges of employees by management. Statements assuring academic freedom were found in 80 per cent of the contracts analyzed by Moskow (1971, p. 51), who finds the subject so much a part of higher education as to be virtually nonnegotiable.

As an issue related to both job security and institutional quality, the merit system needs special consideration. Wollett (1971), addressing himself to salary and load differences, notes that universities need to attract and retain professional faculty members (including doctors, lawyers, and engineers) who are part of a larger market extending beyond the academy, and that universities often prescribe lighter work loads and larger salaries for professional faculty than for other faculty groups (including the liberal-arts and humanities faculty). Separate bargaining units might be developed for such groups. Wollett further comments (p. 18): "It seems unlikely that the majority will long tolerate adverse differentials. . . . Collective-bargaining agents tend to form policies that treat all employees alike." Salary differentials are widely known, but faculty members do not at present make decisions that create them. Collective bargaining could allow faculty members to vote for or against continuing support for a differentiated salary scale based on discipline. Wollett also believes that merit systems are likely to give way to mechanical or quantitative standards applied so as to encourage uniformity—for instance, equal hours of work plus seniority plus equal credits toward an advanced degree means equal pay. The merit system in a state system is in double jeopardy if collective bargaining is state-wide. To avoid unrealistic situations, faculty members would probably have to voluntarily support specialty-related salary differentials, unequal work loads, and a merit system that allows evaluation of individual performances.

THREE MAIN BARGAINING AGENTS

Choosing the bargaining agent that can best represent the unit requires careful thought and a great deal of political maneuvering. Today three major professional organizations represent faculty as bargaining agents. In 1971, of the eighty-one colleges with collective bargaining, forty-one have selected the National Education Association (NEA); thirty, the American Federation of Teachers (AFT); and six, the American Association of University Professors (AAUP).

For sixty years the National Education Association has been primarily associated with elementary and secondary schools. Within the university, the NEA is known primarily in colleges of education; and even there the NEA has not found much support from the faculty interested in higher education. Nevertheless, the NEA represents the largest number of colleges and universities, primarily community colleges, in the collective-bargaining process. Currently it defines its role as having three parts: to organize and coordinate higher education nationally, particularly providing legislation at the federal level;

to strengthen state education associations, resources, and commitment to higher education; and to organize and strengthen campus affiliates by providing staff and resources to do the job —whether it be bargaining, grievance solving, or providing a sufficient voice in campus affairs (Scully and Sievert, 1971).

The American Federation of Teachers was organized nationally in 1916 and affiliated with the American Federation of Labor three years later. Until very recently, the AFT worked primarily with the secondary schools; but recently it has expanded its activities in higher education and established a separate college division. Of the thirty campuses where AFT locals are bargaining agents, twenty-two are two-year colleges. The AFT takes the following position on major issues: that faculty shall determine curriculum, academic standards, and admission standards; elect chairmen; and advise and consent in the selection of chancellors, presidents, and deans; that tenure shall be conferred after a probationary period of not less than one year and not more than four years; and that no disciplinary action, nonrenewal of contract, discharge, or reduction of benefits shall be made without just cause and full due process. The primary strength of the AFT is its experience as a bargaining agent (Scully and Sievert, 1971).

The American Association of University Professors, founded in 1915, has served the faculty search for identity in the framework of higher education. Early objectives of the AAUP included protection of academic freedom and the development of college teaching as a profession. Despite its many activities, the association's concentration on academic freedom and tenure has led many observers to equate the AAUP solely with this effort. At present, groups within the AAUP are debating whether the association should remain primarily a professional organization or become a bargaining organization concerned with economic objectives. The AAUP, with about 100,000 members, is having difficulty determining a single association position on collective bargaining (*Academe,* June 1971). Rather than being able to state specific positions on collective bargaining, the AAUP is concerned with its role—for example, how it can retain its commitments to shared authority among all constituents of the academic world while organizing along the lines of labor versus management, how it can compete with other organizations when it does not admit nonacademic members, how it can preserve its role as arbiter of sensitive issues of academic freedom and tenure and at the same time bargain collectively.

PRESIDENT'S ROLE

One of the most difficult issues in collective bargaining is the role of an institution's chief executive officer. Bertram H. Davis, general secretary of the AAUP, contends that the president's leadership role is supported by delegated authority from both board and faculty. Essentially, this view is built upon the concept of "shared authority," in which both faculty and administration participate and influence decision making, and the president has a dual responsibility as mediator between the faculty and the governing board (Scully and Sievert, 1971).

The American Federation of Teachers strongly opposes the concept of the president's dual role. His emerging role, according to a former president of AFT, is limited to advising and negotiation for the board. This position is based upon the management-labor conflict-of-interest approach, similar to that found in industry. Despite the desires of some presidents to play a dual role, some faculty organizations have made it clear that they do not view the president as their leader in collective bargaining. Although some presidents are still acting in a dual capacity, others are beginning to perceive the inherent conflict of interest. State legislation could, of course, make this issue moot by defining the president's role as the chief administrative officer.

An alternative is for faculty members to negotiate directly with the board, rather than with the president. They are then dealing with the final authority to approve any agreement. However, the board is usually less aware of academic traditions than the president, and this can work to the faculty's disadvantage.

FACULTY'S ROLE

The faculty's role in collective bargaining is even more complicated. "It is clear that one of the fundamental tensions between the faculty and the managers of the educational enterprise springs from the dual role occupied by faculty as members of a profession and as employees" (McHugh, 1971). The concept of professionalism as opposed to unionism dramatizes the freedom and equality conflict. Younger faculty members are coming to regard the appeal to professionalism as ritualistic, while some faculty who support collective bargaining see it as a way to maintain professional ideals that are being corrupted, distorted, and enfeebled. The issue is whether collective-bargaining activities are inconsistent with professional conduct and thus unbecoming to a member of the community of scholars, or whether such activity is necessary in order to establish economic equality and protect jobs. Nowhere is the conflict between professionalism and collective bargaining more clearly drawn than in the question of the strike. Some critics suggest that the use of strikes shifts the basis for professionalism from common commitment and moral entitlement to a power play in a competitive contest, and threatens the existence of shared or cooperative decision making. The countervailing view asserts that teachers are required to practice their profession in the role of an employee. Under these circumstances they cannot control their own wages, hours, and working conditions as do other professionals who are self-employed. The traditional counteractions available to management in a strike situation—lockout and cooperative agreements—also appear unsuitable in higher education.

Some differences between professions and occupations (Miller, 1959, p. 53) were identified by Brandeis in 1912: First, a profession is an occupation for which the necessary and preliminary training is intellectual in character, involving knowledge and to some extent learning as distinguished from mere skill. Second, it is an occupation which is pursued largely for others and not merely for one's self. Third, it is an occupation in which the amount of financial return is not the accepted measure of success. Professors sometimes feel strongly that they are professionals and fear that if they enter into formal collective bargaining, they may become teachers and lose the full dimensionality of their status (Wollett, 1969, p. 1017). To these professors, professional autonomy is directly related to professional self-government. A central theme of collective-bargaining decisions is the nature of a "community of scholars." Who belongs? Who represents them? What freedoms do they have? By moving to a collective-bargaining model, the faculty member could lose some traditional roles. Whether an established grievance procedure, economic advancement, and better working conditions outweigh the values of collegiality and professionalism may depend upon the age of the person answering the question; students and junior faculty members do not see the world in the same light as tenured members.

END OF FACULTY GOVERNANCE?

Lieberman (1971) has concluded that faculty organization for collective bargaining will put an end to faculty self-government. Management and accountability consequent to an agreement will reduce faculty autonomy in most critical decision areas. Representational bodies like faculty senates will have a difficult time holding on to any of their present power. The survival of faculty senates is threatened by conflicts that arise when administrators are members of faculty senates, when organic laws bind the faculty senate to a governing board, and when senates are not self-supporting (Wollett, 1971, pp. 24–25).

Those who support collective bargaining sometimes prefer a reduced faculty role in governance, arguing that self-government has generally been ineffective on the most critical issues. Others believe that since self-government through the traditional methods has been ineffective, collective bargaining is also doomed to fail. The American Association of Higher Education Task Force Report *Faculty Participation in Academic Governance* (1967) suggests that "relationships between the faculty and academic administrators should be, to the greatest feasible extent, collegial rather than hierarchical." Others who have written on the subject (Williams, 1968; Mc-

Connell, 1969) believe that collective bargaining will create greater competition between faculty and administrators. They claim that a strike is not possible and therefore not creditable in negotiations. (Whether they would still hold this view is uncertain; in the current scene, strikes appear quite possible and indeed have happened.)

If faculty senates are to survive collective bargaining, new bylaws will have to be adopted to define membership, establish new relationships with governing boards, and provide for funding. Even so, the representational character of the senate may prove to be its fatal weakness; for senates typically have been dominated by the senior faculty.

IMPACT ON STUDENTS

Much has been written recently about the impact of collective bargaining on faculty and administration, but little has been written on the impact of collective bargaining on students. With some minor exceptions, experience to date has indicated that students have little disposition to use the process. However, several developments suggest that students will become increasingly aware of the collective-bargaining process and will use it to influence matters that directly or indirectly affect their self-interest. Recently the National Students Association voted to build a national union of students (Sievert, 1971). However, a Michigan court has denied collective bargaining rights to hospital interns and residents as separate groups (*Chronicle of Higher Education,* Feb. 7, 1972, p. 9). Faculties will probably introduce into the bargaining process an increasing number of matters that directly affect students (class size, faculty work load, and student membership on university committees). At City University of New York the attempt to place students on university promotion and tenure committees was questioned by the Legislative Conference, which maintained that this attempt constituted a change in the employer-employee relationship. The current state of student-university relations indicates increased student participation in matters once considered prerogatives of the faculty, as well as in administrative policy matters. Feinsinger and Roe (1971), appraising the Teaching Assistants Association (TAA) dispute of 1969–70 at the University of Wisconsin, are convinced that questions of whether teaching assistants wish to bargain collectively have been replaced with questions about the scope of negotiations.

Several difficulties with student participation in collective bargaining should be noted. First, most statutes controlling labor relations concern only the employer-employee relationship. Except possibly in the case of graduate assistants, no such relationship generally exists between students and the university. Second, the transitory nature of students, often discussed in the context of their participation in academic governments, presents unique difficulties for the collective-bargaining model, with its reliance upon units that share a community of interests.

If the student is viewed as a consumer, supporting the efforts of favored teachers, his ability to select courses gives him decision-making power. But if the student is seen as having limited choice in an educational monopoly, then he needs representation in decision-making procedures as well as the ability to select. If students feel that they have no power to influence decisions that affect them (as apparently the NEA students do), then they have a constitutional right to organize. Finkin (1971), Brown and Kugler (1970), Sumberg (1970), and others have commented on the growing involvement and changing role of students. Moskow (1971, p. 40) discusses the scope of collective bargaining in higher education: "Student participation will affect both the structure and scope of collective bargaining in higher education. . . . Student attempts to participate in decisions previously made unilaterally by the administration will encourage faculty involvement as well, thus enlarging the scope of bargaining between faculty and administrator." In particular, proposals to replace direct support of institutions by grants or loans to students would give great force to the student voice. Faculty union proposals to change the educational program or force an increase in tuition and fees would have to reckon with those who pay the bill.

UNIONIZATION AND DEPARTMENTAL AUTONOMY:
THE CASE OF CUNY

As to the effect of collective bargaining or unionization on academic departments, a great deal depends upon the range of considerations that enter into the bargaining process, in addition to the traditional issues of wages, hours, and working conditions. If salaries are negotiated by rank, degree, and number of years of service, without subjective appraisal of merit by administrators, then it is clear that departmental autonomy has been reduced. One can hardly imagine, however, a situation in which all faculty of a university are paid at the rate of those in the medical school or that the medical school faculty's salaries are reduced to the rates of others. Policies for promotions and tenure might also be negotiated so that no room would be left for institutional or departmental decisions. This could impose uniformity upon departments and colleges to an undesirable degree.

At City University of New York, the autonomy of the department was preserved by the Legislative Conference, not in a union contract. Many rules and regulations claimed by the union contracts had been a part of the bylaws of the board for many years, but the interpretation of those bylaws is now a matter for negotiation under conditions of contract violations, rather than decision by chairmen or deans.

The impact of such negotiation is most obvious in connection with continuation of appointments and the granting of tenure. Traditionally universities, acting usually through departmental recommendations, could control the percentage of faculty acquiring tenure. At CUNY the American Federation of Teachers represents faculty members not in the tenure pattern, but bargaining has established nontenure employees in contractual arrangements that are beginning to be stronger than tenure itself. After a person has served five years as a lecturer, his sixth appointment carries with it an administrative certificate of continuous employment. He can be discharged only if a program is phased out, if it can be proved that he has performed unsatisfactorily, or if there is a demonstrated lack of financial ability to continue support of the program at past levels. For those not on continuing contract, appointments must be made for a full year, and dismissal after the first year must be supported by unsatisfactory evaluations for two of the previous three semesters. The effect is that frequently lecturers are routinely given unsatisfactory ratings, to protect departments from having to offer them a continuing contract. The department chairman is in the unhappy position of having to initiate unsatisfactory ratings on faculty members who are performing satisfactorily.

Teaching assistants are placed in a particularly difficult position. If they are held long enough as teaching assistants, they accumulate time which is credited to their continuing or tenure status. Department chairmen tend to give these teaching assistants bad evaluations to avoid their accumulating credits that would assure continuous employment. The university is opposed to hiring its own graduates; but if they continue to hold graduate assistantships and to receive satisfactory ratings before they receive their degrees, continuing appointment may be required. During the transition to the union contract, for example, there was a rash of firing teaching assistants who had been with the system for four years to avoid "grandfathering" them into the system.

The Legislative Conference at CUNY has a board of governors elected for a three-year term, corresponding to the life of the union contract. In general, they deal with issues of wages, hours, and working conditions. During the three-year period they serve as a center for faculty grievances, of which the most common is a failure to be granted tenure on the basis of merit and institutional needs. In deciding whether or not to take a grievance, the Legislative Conference does not sit in academic judgment but rather looks for contract violation. Although in many universities, tenure is often restricted because of the need to limit the size of the tenured faculty, prevent inbreeding, or maintain a proper range of specialties in the tenured faculty, still, departmental autonomy is restricted when such decisions can be regarded as a grievance.

The union negotiates directly with the New York Board of Education, and the middle management of the university is not involved. Because of the contract all chairmen are now elected and thus have become representatives of their faculty rather than interpreters and enforcers of university policy. Because of the contract the chairman's power has been significantly reduced in areas of appointments, scheduling, dismissals, and salaries. A chairman's ability to survive and create an effective department under these conditions depends almost entirely on his individual style, personality, and tactful exercise of influence. Some department chairmen can use the contract and negotiations to learn more about their faculty and to get additional resources. Others are so intimidated by the system that they become at most an executive secretary for their faculty.

Traditionally, university decision making belongs to the governing board and the administration and, in varying degrees, to faculty councils. Typically, faculty councils have considered policies in regard to scholarship, admission, curriculum requirements, hiring, and qualifications of faculty. The union seeks greater democratizing of university governance and the breakdown of artificial distinctions between tenured and non-tenured faculty. Evaluation of faculty must be in line with due process. It is the responsibility of the union to get the board to delineate terms and conditions and to establish a grievance procedure. Subjective judgments of individual performance and individual interpretation of policies are regarded as nonuniform, possibly biased, and hence unfair to individuals. Yet, as faculty members commonly contend when evaluation of their efforts is proposed, completely objective performance criteria are almost impossible to find. Insistence upon publicly presentable and defensible evidence might result in failure to make critical and probably controversial decisions.

University actions on other matters are likely to be impeded by collective bargaining. For example, at present the CUNY institutions are suggesting that student representatives become voting members of all committees, but this means that students could vote on promotion and tenure actions for faculty, which would violate the established contract. At present, the Legislative Conference representing the faculty is fighting this move. The Legislative Conference is also concerned that similar procedures be used in all CUNY institutions. Much of their time is spent on equating differences among institutional practices.

Under collective bargaining a high degree of uniformity

will probably develop in salary patterns that are based upon degrees, rank, and years of service. Uniformity leaves no room for merit recognition and hence no incentive for a faculty member to do more than is required. Typically the quality of departments has varied greatly across a university, but enforced uniformity in salaries is likely to bring all to the same level of distinction—or mediocrity. Desirable variations in institutional quality in public systems of higher education probably require that salaries not be dictated throughout a system, but collective bargaining is likely to move to highest level of control and make it difficult to preserve institutional differences in character and quality. Collective bargaining, if the expectations indicated here are realized, may more effectively curtail departmental autonomy than any other means thus far attempted.

At CUNY, a conflict in aims between the union and the board is illustrated by reactions to the board's desire to award tenure to only 50 per cent of the faculty and no more than 75 per cent in any given department. This fluid level would provide more flexibility in staffing and decrease the budget requirements by permitting the university to recruit new personnel at the lower salary. This proposal was opposed by the Legislative Conference on the ground that it would permit the university to destroy the prospects of junior faculty to advance according to ability. Ultimately the autonomy of the university is threatened when internal pressures and agreements no longer permit adjustment to budgetary realities.

A problem arises from the unwillingness of some deans, chairmen, or senior faculty to make observations and collect information about junior faculty and then to hold regular constructive discussions with them about their performance and their interaction with colleagues. When such discussions are delayed until salary, promotion, or tenure is in question, exchanges that might otherwise be constructive may produce grievances.

Collective bargaining will surely increase job security, but it is likely to make the enforcement of faculty responsibility and ethics even more difficult. The individual who meets the letter of the contract in load and other obligations will be very difficult to displace if he insists on what he conceives to be his rights and exhausts every route of appeal. Although individual evaluations may be agreed upon in a contract, this condition does not necessarily benefit even the capable individual. As we have pointed out, a career can be harmed when unsatisfactory ratings must be used to avoid continuing appointment or tenure. Thus far, unions do not seem to be sensitive to the career problems of individuals beyond the jurisdiction of the local bargaining unit.

As collective bargaining inevitably extends the range of its concerns in an institution, such items as travel expenses to meetings, office hours, sabbatical leaves, consulting for fees, absence from the classroom, as well as teaching load, may become the subject for specific agreements. The autonomy of departments and of the university in making decisions about these matters will disappear and so will the opportunity of discriminating among individual faculty members in extension of these benefits. And with this increased uniformity in rewards and loads, the faculty member's role will probably shift from that of a reasonably autonomous professional to that of a salaried employee with predetermined assignments in which the minimal performance assures continuing appointment—a typical civil service bureaucratic role.

CONCLUSIONS

From this examination of procedures and issues of collective bargaining we have concluded the following:

Higher education is closer to accepting collective bargaining than many believe. Interventions into departmental and university autonomy, tight budgets, and demands for increased faculty teaching loads will accelerate the trend. Faculty members should begin to consider the sort of organization they want to represent their interests. The choice lies to a large degree between an organization that cherishes traditions and one that has experience as a tough negotiator. The "haves" (tenure, position, and high salary) tend to prefer the former; the "have nots," the latter.

University administrators lack experience and usually

continue to act on a collegial base. Many of them are "haves," cherish freedom, and do not listen to demands for equality. This posture, buttressed by inexperience, allows unions to make great initial gains and win swift support.

Collective bargaining upsets the role of middle management. Faculty salary and load differences can be maintained when department, college, and university middle managers make decisions about wages, hours, and working conditions. When such decisions are made by the entire faculty and by direct faculty negotiations with the board, it is doubtful that freedom to maintain reasoned imbalances will remain.

Almost certainly, collective bargaining in higher education will move to state-wide or system-wide levels and in the process destroy much of the autonomy of the separate campuses. Thus, collective bargaining in a state system of higher education will ultimately promote centralization of decision making. Collective bargaining will contravene the individual and departmental autonomy for which many faculty members have battled so long.

6

Governance and Management

In contrast with universities elsewhere in the world, academic governance in the United States has had several distinguishing features. First, the president has, at least until recently, played a decisive role. Second, lay boards are legally responsible for the operation of both public and private institutions. Third, in public institutions the members of the legislature and the state executive offices have a major impact on the governance of institutions through appropriation of funds and review of budget requests; major donors, alumni, and other groups have played a similar role in private institutions. Fourth, a strong central university government has been maintained in accordance with the role played by the president (Graubard and Ballotti, 1970, pp. 108–109). The first and the fourth of these features have been undergoing change as faculty and (more recently) students have sought power. Coincidentally, boards, legislatures, and executive of-

110

ficers have demonstrated increasing tendencies to intervene in institutional governance. One reason for such intervention is that the weakening of administrative authority can lead to inefficient management.

Among several problems to be resolved, two major ones are, first, internal governance and management involving students, faculty, and administrators; and second, external pressures impinge upon internal governance and management. Some major issues involved in governance and management are (1) integration of university goals, management practices, and individual needs; (2) distribution of power and its attendant responsibilities; (3) identification, management, and resolution of conflicts—both within and outside the university; (4) adaptation of governance, management, administration, and organization to the changing social scene within and outside the university; (5) continuing self-examination by the university in a manner which models its expectations for its students (learning how to continue learning, being self-analytical, using evidence to modify behavior). These are difficult issues. The last one is perhaps the hardest and the most important, for it is clearly the inability of the university to examine and direct itself that has led others to try to do so.

As long as universities remained relatively small, insulated from society, concerned with a search for truth, the university was reasonably free to go its own way and develop whatever pattern of governance and management seemed appropriate. Today, as university structures move from unitary to complex and composite, and the university community becomes a megalopolis, these old patterns are inappropriate. In smaller, more compact institutions most faculty members can maintain an identity and involvement; university governance can be, and often is, authoritarian—dominated by a patriarchal or avuncular figure, who may nevertheless be approachable as a human and humane figure. But in the more complex university even an autocratic government becomes something of an oligarchy. As departments, colleges, and institutes grow and proliferate, decision making on minor issues shifts to those units while the university retains strong administrative centralization only on major issues. But faculty members and minor administrators, not entirely satisfied with the funds and prerogatives which seep down to them, demand more and more involvement in major decisions.

In recent years certain developments—for instance, the availability of external funds directly to faculty members and departments, the influence of the AAUP, and the decentralization resulting from increasing size—have combined to give faculty an increasingly stronger voice in governance. In some institutions a distinctive separation of power between central administration and faculty has developed; faculty decide all academic matters, while central administrative offices are concerned primarly with external policies, fund raising, and management. For some faculty members autonomy and academic freedom have become completely separated from academic responsibility. Extremists (Searle, 1971) would abolish boards and turn all authority over to the faculties.

Faculty members have sometimes supported student protest by taking positions that negated effective administrative action. But students have not yet fully realized that power on campus is widely distributed and that many of their concerns are not within the prerogatives of central administration. If the trend for student participation in decision making continues, faculty power will suffer more than administrative power, for much of student concern is directed to matters that are largely the province of the faculty. Both graduate and undergraduate students have been involved in the search for power. Graduate students have been doubly jeopardized through their employment as teaching assistants in the same departments in which they seek a degree. In some respects, the claim of graduate students to participation in governance is even more valid than that of the undergraduates since graduate students are more mature and often serve as instructors or administrators.

The diffused decision-making procedures in universities even as early as ten or fifteen years ago were causing difficulties. The impact of recent events on the universities—outside research support, involvement in studies of social problems and action, discontent with undergraduate programs, faculty and student demands for involvement in governance—has weakened institutional management. A decision-making model in which administrative officers carry out faculty-determined policy runs counter to the expectations of the board, which assumes that administrators carry out board-determined policy. The problem is made more complex by the occasional faculty member who individually interprets policy and expects administrative interpretation to agree.

The administrative organizational pattern itself is confused. It is largely vertical in nature but complicated by the addition of units outside the department and college structure which draw upon individuals within departments or hire people without the usual academic ranks. The question of how to administer such units and how their "faculty" members should be regarded is still unresolved in many universities. The faculty, and more recently the students, have been primarily concerned with the continuity of the university community, including rights and privileges of individuals within it. But today the widespread concern about issues generated outside university walls strongly impinges upon the university and highlights its internal confusion.

External agencies no longer believe that faculty and administrators can be trusted to adjust or control their own vested interests to fulfill their obligations to the public. Moreover, the various groups within the university—students, junior faculty, senior faculty, administrators, clerical, service, and managerial staff—no longer fully trust each other. In general, faith in people has been replaced by faith in rules, codes, and procedures. Respect and cooperation is replaced by distrust and confrontation. Shared authority in the collegial sense, once the goal of most factions on the campus, is gradually being replaced by a sharing of authority based on confrontations and threats of nonperformance of duties until satisfaction is achieved. Both private and public institutions are caught up in this pattern, for private institutions can no longer refuse to negotiate with their students or with appropriately certified employee organizations.

In the face of such reactions, the university is losing its

autonomy and so is everyone within it. Administrative authority is ground away by internal and external intervention and
recalcitrance. The professional wisdom and ethics of the faculty,
individually and collectively, is challenged by students, doubted
by administrators, and negated by the actions of individuals
and groups within the faculty itself.

There is no simple answer as to how a university should
be organized and governed. Ideally, answers should emerge
from clarification of goals and purposes, but this approach is
negated by the university's inability to clarify or even agree
upon its goals. Individuals and departments resist all but the
broadest statement of goals lest the statement exclude their own
aspirations and restrict their activities. In a recent discussion of
university goals by a faculty committee, two statements were
rejected: The first assigned two-year programs to community
colleges; the second stated that no new program would be initiated until funds were specifically appropriated for it. Objec-
tors pointed to programs dear to their own hearts that would
be excluded by the statements.

The people involved in governance are as important as
the structure of governance. Faculty members, students, and
administrators seem to have a hard time keeping in mind the
people outside the university who are involved in its governance. State executives and the legislature have an obvious
input into decision making through budget review and appropriation. Public officials, as well as private citizens, have impact
on university decisions in several ways. Special interest in an
individual student's admission or success alters decisions more
frequently than university administrators would care to admit
publicly. Alumni may also play a very important role in decision making, as more than one president has found when he
has tried to deemphasize intercollegiate sports.

Faculty members tend to assume that the nature of the
university requires that the academic faculty exercise the major
role in decision making. They seldom consider that certain decisions might more properly be made by students or by other
personnel within a university. In fact, some nonacademic university staff members contribute more to the university char-

acter and public image than many faculty members. As these university groups have unionized and bargained collectively for salary or wages, fringe benefits, and other privileges, it has become clear that they have a potent voice. If university decision making is to recognize individual needs, all groups must have a voice, speak to relevant university purposes, and have appropriate degrees of influence.

Although many individuals and groups take part in governance, legally the full responsibility for a university rests with its board. Board members are often considered external, but they are officially a part of the university and provide a major connection between the university and the general public. A strong board can have a crucial role in interpreting the university to the public and in shielding the university from unreasonable incursions into its autonomy. Board subcommittees meeting with deans, departments, or other groups in a university can be of assistance in encouraging faculty and minor administrators to take account of the broader university concerns. Such involvement also gives the faculty and students confidence that their views are known and taken into account in decisions. Yet the active involvement of board members in campus activities is a dangerous practice. Board members are sometimes not sensitive to differences between faculty, students, and the hired help in their own enterprises. Board committee interaction with students and faculty may encourage individual board members to challenge or ignore the presidential role. Elected or appointed boards for public institutions may be inclined to play politics, especially when they have limited insights into higher education. Nevertheless, legal authority is vested in the board; and faculty members assume a difficult role when they try to abridge the authority of a board.

UNIVERSITY GOALS AND GOVERNANCE

Basic university purposes do not give much guidance in priorities for decision making. This is true whether purposes are limited to the traditional trinity (instruction, research, and public service) or augmented by such diverse items as preparation of specialized personnel and babysitting the nation's youth.

Within these broad purposes, one can justify almost any cher-
ished program or activity. But these purposes also include societal responsibilities, and the extent to which the university
fulfills them depends upon the extent to which society will
support universities. Both faculty and students find this a little
difficult to accept; each group expects support for its own thing;
neither is adept at ordering priorities or eliminating programs
when available funds are inadequate.

Because of this insensitivity to social obligations, the advancement of the institution itself may become a major purpose
of decision making. According to Gross (1971), faculty put high
priority on these goals: maintaining academic freedom, increasing the prestige of the university, and maintaining top quality
in programs that faculty members consider especially important. Also, faculty members rate research goals among their
seven most important goals. Administrators give high priority
to these same goals. Commenting on these findings, Gross (p.
47) notes: "By and large the split which many people have become alarmed about . . . does not find support from our data.
The faculty and administrators tend to see eye to eye. . . .
Higher administrators tend to agree with the faculty quite as
much as do lower administrators or chairmen." Similarly, in
The Confidence Crisis we found administrators and faculty
collaborating to acquire funds to advance their institution's
national prestige and disregarding the institution's social obligations. Institutional prestige is based heavily on values
dominated by research, publication, graduate programs, and
departmental autonomy. But not all faculty members or students accept these values; and the conflict generates, in part,
the demand for greater participation in decision making. Personal aspirations are also prominent in the minds of many who
demand participation in governance. Many persons who demand a role in governance do so with purposes unrelated to the
underlying purposes of the university. Wittingly or unwittingly,
they seek to divert the university to achieve individual ends.

Besides the university's expressed goals, several types of
power and influence also affect the formulation, interpretation,
and management of university policy. First, there is the formal

power of assigned or delegated authority. The vertical pyramid of delegated authority is not acceptable in a social institution in which many individuals who carry the burden of work are professionals and are (in their own special field) more competent than anyone higher in the pyramid. Professional competence is a second type of power that influences decision making. Recognition of an individual as an expert makes it difficult to avoid accepting his recommendation. Faculty members sometimes forget, however, that expertise in one field does not qualify an individual as an expert on all university problems. Governance and management in the university is a continuing search for an appropriate accommodation among individuals, each of whom claims to be an authority in his own specialty as well as in university administration.

A third type of power is that of the purse. In private and public universities, the offer or the denial of funds profoundly influences university decisions. A fourth type of power arises out of the university's sensitivity to bad publicity. Faculty members and students have noted this sensitivity and used it to personal advantage. Confrontations, sit-ins, and the like, have been found by students to be effective ways of forcing compromise or capitulation.

A fifth type of influence on university decisions is sentiment and emotion. Personal concerns about an individual and his family, rather than professional judgment of competency, sometimes are reasons why obvious incompetents are retained. Faculties are generally unwilling to discipline their own recalcitrants and incompetents—because of some mixture of compassion, reluctance to be involved in difficult decisions, and toleration (even admiration) of professorial idiosyncrasies.

There are other less obvious but highly significant weapons in exerting power. One who controls the sources of information and reveals only what he wishes can promote the decisions he desires. Secrecy itself is a potent factor in decision making; for when decisions are made in secret and kept secret, decisions can be made which might not stand up under public examination. But the process of public examination exacts a toll; subjected to political influence and administrative review, truly innovative ideas may be watered down or lost. Change may be vetoed by individuals in power or by power blocs. Deference to faculty seniority is similar to that in the legislature. If protracted debate, parliamentary maneuvering, and detailed examination of all points of view must precede action, progress can be thwarted. Indeed, students and younger members of the faculty—seeing university governance in action for the first time—are invariably surprised, distraught, or disillusioned by what they find.

The university decision-making process focuses largely on the development of policies, with little or no regard for policy management—that is, interpretation and enforcement. Frequently the attempt to interpret and enforce a policy simply starts a chain of events in which the policy itself is ultimately reexamined. Faculty and students demand such individual attention that it is difficult for administrators to enunciate an unambiguous policy and much of their energy is dissipated on interpretation and enforcement.

One may learn much about where power lies by asking such questions as the following: (1) Who assigns the work to the faculty and other personnel? (2) Who determines the criteria of good performance? (3) Who collects and organizes the evidence from which decisions about performance are to be made? (4) Who makes decisions about the rewards (money, status, amount of independence, public recognition)? (5) Who can change the university—its purposes, its organizational structure, or its priorities? One can tell much about the power in a university by determining who interprets policies and by examining whether changes in the university are brought about by an administrator, the board, or by manipulation of the reward system.

If, as the vice-chancellor of an English university said, a professor or department chairman can be an emperor presiding over his domain, it is equally true that presidents have dominated their colleges or universities. However, it would be an oversimplification to assume that simply because a single individual exercises a major leadership role in an institution, its governance is authoritarian. There have been and probably still are some institutions where presidents make practically all decisions, including promotions and salary adjustments. In some cases the president also wears a cloak of religious authority. A somewhat more flexible person plays an avuncular role. John A. Hannah, the long-time president of Michigan State University, was widely known for moving the institution forward in great strides during his presidency and at the same time was widely respected for his vision and willingness to undertake innovation on a moment's notice. Despite his dominant role, he was interested in individuals and accessible to them. In other institutions which have had a single, strong president for some years, the governance actually has been more of an oligarchy, with some members of the oligarchy not always visible. Today, most universities have simply become too complicated to be dominated by one or by a few people. One university in our case studies had a total of thirteen individuals carrying "vice-president" or "provost" in their title. By the time an organization becomes that complicated, the chief administrator is effectively walled off from operating units.

THREE PATTERNS OF GOVERNANCE

The complicated structure of today's university involves patterns of university governance which may be described as bureaucratic, collegial, or political.

Bennis (1971, p. 542) characterizes the bureaucratic style in the university as an impersonal pattern with (1) a well-defined chain of command, rules, practices, or procedures covering practically all contingencies that may occur; (2) an assignment or assumption of tasks based upon special competencies; (3) promotion and selection based upon these technical competencies; and, as a result of all of these characteristics, (4) a strong tendency toward impersonality in human relations. It is unlikely that the true bureaucratic model has ever functioned in any university. University purposes do not define products in sufficient detail to assign specific tasks, control work load, or set performance standards for research and classroom duties. Many bureaucracies include highly trained professionals more competent than their superiors in the chain of command, and tensions result. This tension occurs between the nonmedical director and the medical staff in hospitals and also in industries when they try to accommodate large groups of scientists.

As the university has grown in size, the concern for democracy, cooperation, and humanistic values rather than a mechanistic, coercive approach has caused the university to search, so far unsuccessfully, for an alternative to the bureaucratic pattern. An inherent weakness of a bureaucracy is its inability to accommodate rapid or unanticipated change.

To some people the term "collegial" invokes visions of a utopia in which university purposes are sufficiently definite and accepted to give individual guidance, and an admiring and awed society assures financial support without demonstrated need or without intervention into university purposes or operations. In this utopia few administrators are needed. A small core of clerical and business assistants would handle day-to-day operations while scholars, on a rotating basis, assume the roles as chairmen, deans, vice-chancellors, or whatever other titles may be in use. Most problems would be settled by departments if not by the individual teacher or researcher. When problems involving the welfare of some larger group are involved, solutions will be found through consensus achieved by committees or town meetings. This utopian concept recognizes neither the complications of the modern university nor the range of activities and personnel it requires. Perhaps slightly less idealistic is the conception of a community of scholars managing its own affairs. This conception accepts that the university has major business and management problems which require specialized administrative skills. However, the university would be devoted to scholarship, and scholars would form a community in which to develop the minimal policies necessary to assure the institution's continued existence. This conception leaves to the individual the greatest possible autonomy in carrying out his self-defined responsibilities.

If professional competence is emphasized, then a somewhat different conception of collegiality may emerge. Since faculty members' specialized professional competency is produced by the graduate training within each discipline, professional competence is shared by a group of people trained in each discipline; collegiality then accommodates the disciplinary-based department as the major decision- and policy-making unit. One difficulty with this conception is that professional competence and disciplinary training have little relevance to several major faculty functions, including curriculum development, instruction, and advising. Competent professionals usually have given little thought to the total undergraduate program in their own discipline and none at all to the general problem of undergraduate education. Thus, collegiality, when based upon current conceptions of professional competence, is consistent only with a conception of undergraduate education in which the student's major field is the primary concern and each department is responsible for its majors.

Like the bureaucratic, the collegial approach assumes that change is not a major concern or problem. Changes come about through individual efforts or through departmental structure that makes decisions only by consensus. In the bureaucracy conflict is controlled by bureaucratic sanction. In the collegial community it is eliminated by respect and trust. But "keeping the faith" ignores students and dissident faculty members who join students in demands for major changes. The collegial approach places much emphasis on human relations among professionals and views the institution as a backdrop for individual performance. A bureaucracy emphasizes execution of policy while the community of scholars emphasizes the formulation of broad, occasionally vague policies which accommodate individual scholarship and professionalism.

Faculties have generally rejected the bureaucratic pattern in the university, but they have not been satisfied with the collegial one. Unanimity in point of view among junior and senior faculty and between faculty, students, and other personnel in the university is lacking. Those who have seen faculty members change their points of view after becoming administrators readily realize that there is a gulf between administrators and faculty members which is not easily bridged. Bureaucracy in the university is as impractical as collegiality is idealistic.

A POLITICAL APPROACH

Conflict is a fact in the university. There is conflict between the humanities and the sciences; between the liberal arts and the professional fields; and among priorities, purposes, and educational objectives. Conflicts are not simply between faculty and administration; some of the most vicious infighting takes place between colleagues in the same department. The fact is that every university has special-interest groups which try to influence policy and attain power. Baldridge (1971, p. 10) has noted and discussed these points and adds several others:

> Small groups of political elites govern most of the major decisions. However, this does not mean that *one* elite group governs everything, but the decisions are divided up with different elite groups controlling different decisions.
>
> Formal authority, as prescribed by the bureaucratic system, is severely limited by the political pressure and bargaining that groups can exert against authorities. Decisions are not [consensual, but neither are they] simply bureaucratic orders. . . . [They are] instead negotiated compromises among competing groups.
>
> External interest groups have a great deal of influence over the university, and internal groups do not have the power to make policies in vacuum.

The political approach recognizes conflict and, rather than attaining consensus, looks for a compromise that no one likes in its entirety but that a majority will support because several minorities find different components acceptable. Baldridge (1971, p. 13) well describes this approach:

> The broad outline of the university's political system looks like this: there is a complex social structure that generates multiple pressures; there are many forms of power and pressure that impinge on the decision makers; there is a legislative stage that translates these pressures into policy; and there is a policy-execution phase that finally generates feedback with the potential for new conflicts.
>
> This approach will bring several factors under close

scrutiny. First, it should be evident that we will be addressing ourselves primarily to problems of *goal setting* and the conflict over values rather than to problems of maximum efficiency in carrying out goals. Second, the analysis of *change processes* and the adaptation of the university to its changing internal and external environment will naturally be a critical part of a political study of university governance. . . . Third, the *analysis of conflict* and conflict resolution must be a critical component of a political study. Fourth, the role that *interest groups* play in pressuring decision makers toward the formulation of certain types of policy must be an important element in the analysis. Finally, much attention should be given to the *legislative and decision-making* phases—the processes by which pressures and power are translated into policy. Taken together, these emphases are the bare outline for political analysis of university governance.

COMPLEXITY OF UNIVERSITY STRUCTURE

The typical university organizational pattern is hierarchical and suggests a bureaucratic pattern. Usually the president is appointed by the board and serves at its pleasure, with all other appointments made upon recommendation of the president. A hierarchical organization runs from the president to several vice-presidents, deans, directors, and department chairmen. This vertical organization is complicated by the existence of centers, institutes, and offices which report horizontally and by individuals who report at different places in the horizontal pyramidal organization. Thus, there exist both a vertical and a horizontal organization.

In some universities all-university departments have been created. Psychology, for example, might normally appear in several colleges; but instead of several different psychology units controlled by various colleges, a single autonomous department with relations to several colleges may be created, as at Syracuse University. Mathematics may also be an all-university department, including pure and applied mathematics, statistics, and computer science. All-university departments may be composed of several units, with each unit assigned to a particular college, or may simply be a multiunit department with the chairman reporting to several deans or to the chief academic officer. Patterns for budgeting of such departments vary. If they have multiple sources of funds, they may acquire more dollars and more autonomy than the typical department.

As universities have moved to centralize services (audiovisual aids, evaluation, and the like), the departments' use of these services is not always reflected in the departmental budget; then departments can build their instructional programs so that a significant percentage of the cost is handled by services budgeted elsewhere. When a university undertakes, as did the University of Oklahoma at one time, to separate the budgeting from the college deans, clearly a vertical and a horizontal pattern have been introduced. Presumably the vertical path is that followed by the dollars.

Another distinction too little used in higher education is that between permanent and temporary units. In large businesses the typical organization is a vertical hierarchy, but for major projects a team may be brought together from units within the institution to serve under a project director for a certain length of time. In a university, an institute set up to carry out research on urban problems is in this pattern. The problem arises in the university when such an institute becomes permanent and hires its own full-time staff. Greater use of temporary organizational patterns would probably be beneficial. Bennis (1971, p. 550) suggests this prospect:

> The social structure of organizations of the future will have some unique characteristics. The key word will be "temporary." There will be adaptive, rapidly changing temporary systems. These will be task forces organized around problems to be solved by groups of relative strangers with diverse professional skills . . . on an organic rather than mechanical model . . . evaluated not vertically acording to rank and status, but flexibility and functionally according to skill and professional training.
>
> Adaptive problem solving, temporary systems of diverse specialists, linked together by coordinating and task-evaluation executive specialists in an organic flux—this is the organizational form that will gradually replace bureaucracy. . . . I call this organic-adaptive structure.

CHANGE IN THE UNIVERSITY STRUCTURE

Achieving the flexibility to shift from vertical to horizontal patterns or from permanent to temporary units will not be easy for most universities. Bureaucracy does not readily adapt to change. However, a strong individual can often bring about change by virtue of his status. For example, in one institution academic titles were conferred only through departments. A prestigious individual who headed a new institute insisted that he could not hire persons he wanted without giving them academic title and tenure. He was unwilling to waste time negotiating with departments and was sufficiently forceful to break the long-existing policy.

Any departure from the typical bureaucratic pattern poses a new complication. The administrator responsible for an innovative pattern may find that his regular responsibilities take up so much of his time that he has little to spare for the new program or that he has relatively little knowledge about the innovation; therefore, he extends even more autonomy to the operation. Faculty members who have appointments in several units may attain a degree of autonomy not common for a person assigned to a single unit, although such an individual runs the risk of being overlooked in the reward structure. A department, like an individual, placed in two or more colleges has the same possibilities and the same risks.

A general guide for those seeking to restructure an institution is that form should follow function. The typical bureaucratic university-college-department pattern functions reasonably well in performing traditional instructional and research activities closely related to the disciplinary structure. But it does not function well for other tasks. Research, service programs, and innovative undergraduate and graduate programs require the formation of task forces in which various specialists are brought together to explore new problems. One might speculate that a pattern could develop in which budgeting is based entirely upon program units such as undergraduate colleges, research institutes, interdisciplinary graduate programs, and public service centers with departments assigned an informal and unbudgeted role in planning courses and curriculums.

Whether truly functional or not, the form of governance is not neutral with respect to the goals and values of higher education. The bureaucratic emphasis is on efficiency and order. In order to measure efficiency objectively, quantitative measures of both input and output are required. Program budgeting, cost effectiveness, and accountability become major concerns. Numbers of degrees awarded, numbers of credit hours produced, numbers of student credit hours or number of credits per full-time-equivalent instructor are typical of the data used for program review, evaluation, and budgeting. On the other hand, the collegial emphasis (the community of scholars) largely ignores efficiency or would measure it in quite different terms than the bureaucratic approach. The collegial emphasis gives precedence to scholarly values: autonomy for the individual; attention to quality rather than quantity; the existence of a scholarly, intellectually challenging environment; and flexibility in adapting faculty assignments and responsibilities to personal needs (and whims).

Practically, the involvement of many groups—faculty, students, administrators—would seem to push the university toward a political or a collective-bargaining model. Either they interact and attempt to resolve their differences and priorities, or they separately bargain with administration or governing boards to attain their goals. Certainly governance on the campus is becoming more political in nature. Concern about who holds the power and how to get a piece of it, or how to influence those who hold it, then becomes the center of attention. Faculty and student groups compete with each other for achievement of special interests and goals, joining forces only in confronting administrators, board members, and external agencies. External coordination and role determination deeply irritates faculty and administrators; for example, in the California state colleges they see the Master Plan discriminating against them in salaries, teaching load, programs, leaves, facilities, and general support. The humanities and to some extent the social sciences feel that they have been cast in an inferior role by the support accorded the sciences. Junior faculty seek quick routes to job security and a voice in deliberations traditionally accorded only to senior faculty. Discontent is rife; and collective bargaining holds attraction for many faculty members, who see it as the only effective recourse against administrative interference with their prerogatives and external intervention into faculty institutional autonomy.

FACULTY SENATES AND COMMITTEES

Every university has an organization bringing together faculty members from all units to meet and discuss institutional problems. The still most common pattern has been a general faculty town meeting chaired by the president or chief academic officer. But as institutions have grown, meetings of the total faculty have become less feasible. Currently, the most common forum is probably a representational senate elected by various constituencies. The problem of defining these constituencies is not easy: temporary and nontemporary faculty would like to be represented; students insist upon it. It is usually unclear whether administrators should be *ex officio* senate members, or officers, or whether any administrators should even be present at meetings. Further complications arise when representation is based upon racial and sexual groupings. If in addition, a multiple-campus university like the University of Minnesota organizes a senate to include representation from the several campuses, the extent to which each senator represents any particular constituency at any given moment is uncertain.

Since much of the work is done through committees, the administrator who appoints committees can influence senate recommendations and actions. Some faculties flatly reject administrative-appointed committees, believing, with some justification, that such committees will make only those recommendations the administrator wants. If committees are elected, they do not necessarily contain the right people to deal with a particular problem and are likely to contain opportunists who seek to advance themselves. Regardless of how they are selected, committee members often spend many sessions clarifying their relationship to other committees, asserting their authority with regard to the particular problem, and demanding assurance that their conclusions will be accepted without referral to some other deliberative group.

University senates and committees (ignoring the often excessive costs in time and energy) can do a reasonably satisfactory job of developing policy and procedural statements. They are not effective as administrative bodies, and they tend to confuse development of policies with their interpretation and administration. As students have joined the deliberations, the decision time has been stretched out until students find they cannot spare the time for endless meetings, or conclude that significant change is impossible by such procedures. This, of course, has happened for years with some faculty members, seriously involved as scholars and teachers, who have refused to give the time required for senate deliberations.

The future of university senates depends upon what happens to universities. In the short-term future the collegial approach is likely to expand and perhaps include student involvement in some matters. At the senate expands, it will find itself, as unions already have, involved in political activity and intervention on the two-way street between the university and the public. We predict that as the senate operating in a collegial pattern attempts to handle issues external to academic concerns (involving admission policies, institutional goals or structure, and so on), it will generate external restrictions (from legislatures, coordinating boards, and others) justified on the grounds that the board, representing the people, is no longer in control.

DECENTRALIZING AND CENTRALIZING TENDENCIES

Change in the university can be viewed in terms of two opposing forces, centralizing and decentralizing, with one or the other dominating in an irregular and unpredictable pattern. Both private and public universities have tended toward decentralization. Increasing institutional size, faculty and student demands for participation, department and college demands for more autonomous budgeting and control of funds—these are some of the pressures for decentralization.

The rotation of chairmen and deans, coupled with

faculty involvement in their selection, creates an additional problem. This practice limits the administrator's ability to use his presumed authority, for its exercise might create difficulties when he has to rotate back into the faculty. Moreover, the rotation of administrators scarcely permits an individual to become acquainted with problems of the office before it is time for him to vacate it. An administrator must have both the ability and the authority to exercise power if he is to be strong enough to fulfill his responsibilities.

The university must have either strong deans or strong chairmen. If both are strong, conflicts may jeopardize progress. If department chairmen are stronger than deans, decentralization may go too far. Thus, strong deans are generally desirable. But if both chairmen and deans cater to the faculty, it becomes virtually impossible to enforce simple and reasonable university policies.

Campus governance or organization which assumes that the institution is being run for the benefit of the faculty rather than of society is doomed to fail. Some balance must be found between centralization and decentralization. This is true within the university; it is true in state systems of universities; and it is true with the whole system of higher education in the United States.

Numerous forces push toward centralization of authority within universities and university systems. Financial stringency is a major one. Whenever it is necessary to cut back appropriations, information is needed to justify the action; the need for information spawns management information systems, and these bring pressures for centralized controls. Financial stringency also raises concern about program duplication and instructional load and reinforces demands for state coordination. Although external support—through grants given to individual projects—obviously contributes to decentralization, in some respects it also contributes to centralization; for as institutions look to the federal government for support, they find themselves pressured into uniform procedures, records, and programs. In the early stages of unionization, where the approach is through single institutions, unionization may not be seen as a pressure toward centralization; but, inevitably, in a state system of higher education, salary comparisons among institutions will force unions to move their efforts to a higher level. Inevitably, unionization itself becomes a force toward centralization, the determination of policies on a system or state-wide basis rather than for a single institution. Legal rulings have also come to be a force for centralization, as students and faculty members have recourse to the courts for redress of grievances against their university. An individual's dissatisfaction with a single institution's policies can, if resolved by court actions, establish precedents or policies which all institutions must accept.

Governance involving extensive student and faculty participation is expensive as well as often ineffective. Some individuals who have been heavily involved in such efforts assert that additional committees simply create more confusion and more committees. Committee work could be reduced if administrators were relied on to formulate and carry out policy, subject to occasional review. Committees and universities generally make too little use of the relevant faculty expertise which exists on the campus. Individuals who serve as consultants to business, industry, and government are seldom called upon to advise in the university.

Participatory democracy in the university becomes especially difficult in times of financial stress, when harsh decisions have to be made. When it is evident that students and faculty demands can be met only if some things are forgone, unpopular decisions perhaps can be made and explained. But hard decisions involving retrenchment are unpopular with administrators as well as with students and faculty.

Several issues emerge from this discussion. The first is the problem of representation in democratic governance. Only those who volunteer or express an interest in senate membership are likely to be elected. Once elected, they will encounter conflicts of interest which involve their own personal aspirations, their department, or their college. If all senators were so motivated, the values which would govern decisions would likely give precedence to departmental aspirations and priorities at the expense of university interests and the society it serves.

Who should be involved, and in what decisions? Should students have certain responsibilities; faculty members, others; the administration, still others? A clear-cut division of labor is probably not possible in the university. Students will probably insist on expressing their views about the investment of university funds, the kind of research done on campus, and the curriculum and instruction provided. Thus in the typical university every group has pervasive concerns about all university problems. At present, we have no evidence that wiser decisions are being made or that faculty members are any more satisfied in institutions with faculty-dominated senates.

A second problem has to do with weaknesses inherent in collective decisions in the university. Government in our society typically has executive, legislative, and judicial agencies. The university may slowly be developing a counterpart of these. However, many faculty members reject a strong executive branch and want more authority for the faculty. This attitude ignores several factors. Change takes place in a university only if new ideas are initiated, accepted, and put into effect. If faculty members reject a proposal simply because it is initiated by administrators, a major source of innovation will have been destroyed. Only limited change can occur when constituent groups hold veto power. Limited changes or additional options may be accepted, but a significant replacement of existing traditions and prerogatives is unlikely. The ultraconservative educational pattern preferred by faculty (many professors are liberal in politics, economics, or religion, but conservative in education) is one argument for retaining a strong central administration. Presidents or other administrators interested in constructive change will do well to listen to individuals and minority groups instead of being influenced mainly by a conservative faculty majority voiced through governance channels.

Another weakness in collective decisions is that responsibility is diffuse; indeed, it is often evaded. Presidents and administrators can be forced to resign when they make mistakes. Just what happens when a senate makes a bad decision is not certain. But one can be very sure that senate members will not resign their professorships or even their senate positions. The collective approach, furthermore, is not likely to make prompt, clean-cut, hard decisions about matters that have very serious impact on the public—matters such as elimination of programs, reduction in costs, violations of professional ethics. No one can foresee all contingencies of a given policy; hence, no policy can be administered effectively unless the administrator has sufficient authority to act in individual cases without approval. The mere fact that a senate has passed a policy statement does not mean it is any more acceptable to individual faculty members than if the policy had been enunciated by the president. No matter how well a policy is stated, no matter how effectively it is communicated to the faculty, there is no assurance that faculty actions will accord with the policy. If an administrator's authority to enforce policy is diluted by faculty sharing of executive and legislative powers, the collective-decision approach will fail.

New faculty and students tend to question policies in which they had no part. This is particularly true in a highly democratic situation, much less true in a situation where major policy statements come from the administration with the board's authority. Another weakness in collective decisions is the general insensitivity of group decisions, which raises the question as to how a faculty member is to be protected against unjust actions by the faculty. Still another weakness is the strong probability that faculty pressures will be toward allocation of all funds into the traditional college and departmental structure. Innovations, university-wide instructional services, counseling, and similar activities would very likely go by the board if decisions were made in a collective fashion.

Another problem is the selection and emerging role of administrators. If all administrators were selected by the faculty and served on a rotational basis, the autonomy of the operating level units would be virtually uncontrolled. Ultimately, budgetary problems, excesses of behavior, and decreases in productivity would probably force external intervention.

The report of the Committee on Higher Education in Britain rationalizes the participation of laymen in governing boards as follows:

More than 85 per cent of the university finance comes from public sources, and in our judgment it is in general neither practical nor justifiable that the spending of university funds should be wholly in the hands of the users. Academic autonomy is more likely to be safeguarded where the public has a guarantee that there is an independent lay advice and criticism within the university. . . . Where men and women of wide experience and high standing in the world of affairs can spare time to associate themselves with university activities, the universities gain from the partnership strength and sagacity in their dealings with the outside world. And, even where academic affairs are concerned, lay arbitration is a valuable resource in case of conflict [McConnell, 1971b, p. 119].

The process of university governance may well be political. It involves a great deal of negotiation and compromise and is probably more legislative and judicial than executive. Faculties have come to have a great deal of power, although much of it is veto power, and may gain more power; but senior faculty members may end up sharing their power with others to a greater extent than they had envisioned. Students will demand a great deal more say in policy making. However, student interests are generally unpredictable; there are some signs that students do not have the time necessary for decision-making processes and are more concerned with eliminating restraints. Clearly, it is the board and the president that are losing authority. They have great responsibility but little power. As a national and world leader, a president may accomplish a great deal, but he has very little control over his university. This is a crucial concern for those who believe the university is out of control.

The idealistic conception of a university consisting of individuals, each guided by his conscience and his sense of academic and scholarly obligations, operating freely without constraints, never was true in any university and certainly is not true in the multiplication of universities and university systems we have in this country. The faculty do not usually impose controls on their associates. When controls are imposed, they come from pressures from students, parents, legislators, and special-interest groups, and then they appear to be unreasonable intervention by the board and the president. Controls for the sake of clerical efficiency ought to be examined carefully. But policy controls are essential for fundamentally efficient and effective university operation. If university governance cannot provide management controls—or, more specifically, if the faculty will neither impose nor permit such controls to be imposed by boards and administrators—then faculty members may expect increasing external control.

In the face of these external pressures, the reconsideration of internal campus governance cannot be overestimated.

> Something on the order of selective decentralization will probably have to take place in the next few years. Indeed we can begin to see the outlines of such a movement on the horizon at the present time with the interest in cluster colleges. . . .
>
> Clearly some way must be found whereby individuals can participate more meaningfully in decision making that governs their own lives. Electing one representative to speak for a body of 20,000 students will not make the 19,999 students satisfied in very many institutions. . . . Those activities which directly touch the lives and futures of individuals should be handled with the smallest possible decision-making machinery, while those matters which are largely purely logistical and have little reference to individual lives should be handled in the largest possible network [Hodgkinson, 1970a, p. 160].

However, many of the concerns of the faculty and other segments of the university in regard to work load and salary benefits and involvement in decisions about these items must be resolved at the university level. And when resources are static or diminishing, there may be no alternative but strong administrations or central-system coordination.

> Since a university is not a parliamentary body, and even less a place where total participation is possible, the existence of a strong executive authority is essential. Only where such authority exists is there any possibility that proposed innova-

tions will be debated, tested, and, when appropriate, imple-
mented.

There is little self-regulation by faculty in most institutions. Only the most flagrant evidence of gross misbehavior
will involve an individual in disciplinary actions initiated by
colleagues. . . . The alternative to such self-regulation may
be a form of additional outside control that carries hazards
for intellectual freedom in the colleges and universities of the
country [American Academy of Arts and Sciences, 1971, p. 10].

The external pressures of the present era upon the university,
the incursions into its autonomy, and the unrest thereby created
in the faculty will almost certainly encourage the development
of collective bargaining. And as collective bargaining continues,
and as each year the range of items subjected to bargaining
increases, bargaining will certainly move to confrontations between boards of trustees and faculty or between coordinating
or control boards and combined faculty unions for a whole
state. In this process the distinction between administrative
authority and faculty rights may become somewhat clearer.
What is even more clear is that unless students organize and
lay demands upon the faculty as well as upon the administration, faculty concerns and priorities may determine what the
university becomes. But if both faculty and students organize,
the university may see more controversy than ever before, and
the character of decision making may change to a pattern of
resolution through continuing confrontation.

7

Planning and
Program Budgeting

The purpose of planning and program budgeting is to achieve the most effective allocation of funds to program categories. It does so by presenting alternatives from which the institution can designate preferred choices, providing a basis for decision by coordinating councils, state executives, and the legislatures. Ideally, planning and program budgeting would make for wiser use of funds at the institutional level and permit the state to designate what it proposes to buy with its dollars. The university would display its wares with a price affixed to each item, and the public could decide what it wants to buy. Ideally, too, it would begin with zero-base budgeting, considering each existing program on its merits (cost effectiveness or cost benefits), and suggest different levels of support and alternative modes of operation and of achieving goals. Costs would be expected to vary; but, unfortunately, so could the effectiveness and the benefits. And for educational

136

programs (yet to be defined) the costs, benefits, and effectiveness are not readily determined so that the cheapest way to offer a particular program could be regarded as the best choice.

Planning and program budgeting is also designed to tie program planning and analysis of program effectiveness directly to budget decisions. Its rationale is that budget decisions determine the support of programs and the priorities among them. Educators will be forced to examine what the university accomplishes and to weigh alternative programs and methods within the budget available. Legislatures will see their task not simply as adjusting budget requests to available income but rather as deciding upon priorities and support levels in relation to available funds and state needs.

Traditional budgeting practices have started with the assumption that the current level of university support establishes a minimal base for the next year's budget, to which are added the funds required for salaries, price-level adjustments, and projected increases in student enrollments or expansion of existing programs. An addend may reflect the need for upgrading or for catching up on past deficiencies in support. Finally, new programs are indicated and the dollars for these are added. The result is the "asking" budget. It might also be described as a planning budget, except that precious little planning is involved. This "asking" budget provides a ceiling for negotiations on an operating budget. Since cuts are expected, the request is inflated.

This traditional practice usually assumes also that the budget request of each college and department is derived much like that of the university as a whole. In fact, a large part of the university request is determined by adding the requests of the subunits. As long as additional funds are forthcoming each year, each department and college is virtually assured of no less support than that of the past year. In practice, university increases usually mean college and departmental increases. If each subunit requested the minimum amount necessary for continuing its present program, there would be little possibility of improvement in quality or range of programs. Even if the university and each subunit obtained exactly what it requested, the university would probably suffer in comparison with other universities proposing requests on an expansionist basis. By encouraging each subunit to express its aspirations, university administrators are in a better position to appraise deficiencies and needs, interpret requested increases, and allocate whatever funds are received. Viewed in this way, requests based on minimums provide less information than those which are in some degree "inflated" by inclusion of aspirations.

This approach to budgeting provides minimal information for external review and prevents direct intervention into internal operations and priorities. It also provides minimal leverage for reallocation of resources within the university. The chief element of flexibility is in the allocation of the new dollars (the increment over last year's budget).

A budgetary agency responsible for initial review of institutional requests can deal systematically with items of salary adjustments, cost increases, or new programs; but is seriously handicapped in any attempt to review the nature of, need for, and pattern of operations of existing programs.

THE NATURE OF PPBS

A program-budgeting approach has two aspects: first, to explain the purposes (or characteristics) of a unit and to relate its income and expenditures to its purposes in a format which displays the contribution of each program's activities to the overall purpose; second, to produce a plan, projected over several years, indicating how purposes may change and how they may be achieved in the future, assessing alternatives and their probable costs and impacts. Whereas the first aspect involves primarily clarification of goals, the second provides the opportunity to move gradually toward more efficient use of resources in attaining these goals.

Planning and program-budgeting systems (PPBS) may impose new structures (curriculum groupings, for example) upon old structures (departments and colleges) to suit a need for comparable programs across educational institutions. PPBS may also involve a set of new analytical procedures applied to budget requests or a new way of presenting budgets so that objectives, educational processes, and expected outcomes can be related to the resources requested.

Program budgeting is effective only if institutions accept it as a tool useful to themselves as well as to those who provide the funds. The planning budget must be differentiated from the actual operating budget, which serves as a management tool. Obligations to faculty (tenure) and to students (opportunity to complete programs in which they are enrolled) make it difficult for a university to modify materially its operations in a single year. Therefore, planning must take place for some period of years in advance. Objectives or goals must be stated, resource requirements projected, and prospective budgets (both operating and capital) estimated. State universities are reluctant or even averse to doing this, and sometimes for very good reasons.

PROBLEMS IN PPBS

Universities find that PPBS is difficult, time-consuming, expensive, and sometimes self-defeating. They are not alone. Prisons, welfare, and conservation agencies also have trouble defining outcomes for program budgets. Many state universities lack sufficient manpower and information to undertake long-range planning while they are preparing next year's request, still defending the current one, and at the same time attempting to finish the current year without a deficit. Planning which entails program eliminations or cutbacks is distasteful, dissension provoking, and intensely enervating because of the time and energy which must be spent in committee discussions, personal conferences, and confrontations. Prominent in the minds of administrators and institutional boards is the fear that a realistic projection involving economies and cutbacks could be both self-fulfilling and institutionally debilitating.

Through its colleges, departments, centers, and institutes, a university develops programs to carry out its functions of instruction, research, and service. A complicating factor is that a department may engage in programs of instruction, research, and public service in such fashion that the three are inextricably related. A demand for reduction in research could destroy a graduate degree program, and the denial of a public-service role could handicap or eliminate a curriculum closely related to the service. Many programs of instruction (medicine, engineering, or undergraduate degrees in the arts and sciences) require the cooperation of several units; so too with research and public service activities. The end products of programs—degrees or social or technological improvements—are the results of collaboration, not readily assigned to a particular unit, not easily costed, and not readily assessable as to benefits. Since budgets typically are developed by and for colleges and departments, a program definition which does not correspond to this structure requires vastly more elaborate procedures and data systems than most universities can currently operate. These difficulties can be overcome, in time, if universities decide that it is to their advantage to cooperate.

A program budget presents three sets of alternatives. One is a choice between very different programs, only one of which can be supported by the resorces in prospect. A liberal-arts college may find that it is able to provide a major in physics or in chemistry; costs in space, equipment, and staff prohibit offering both. A university may decide that it can no longer support professional programs in law, medicine, and dentistry. Which does it eliminate? No solution may be acceptable to all interested parties, but the availability of these programs in other nearby institutions is an important consideration. Such choices are not new, but the program-budget approach—emphasizing long-term planning and choice among alternatives by reference to projected benefits and financial constraints—affords a more systematic way of dealing with them.

The second and third sets of alternatives present choices within rather than between programs. For example, a program in policy administration which is growing beyond available resources may be reexamined and several possibilities considered in a "decision packet": (1) restriction to the junior and senior students; (2) reduction in number of professional courses and the use of large lecture sections; (3) elimination of field work; (4) limitation on the number of students admitted; (5) continued expansion, provided necessary resources can be ob-

tained; and (6) elimination of the program. Each of these hypo-
thetical possibilities affects costs and poses certain issues of
quality and of public service.

The second alternative is a choice between processes or
means by which a program's purpose (preparing individuals for
various types of protective service) is accomplished (restriction
to the junior and senior years, eliminating field work). The
third alternative is a choice between levels of support: in the
example, determining the number of students, social agencies,
businesses, and police departments whose needs can be accommodated. The university should present its preferred alternative
based on educational grounds and on its assessment of needs.
A coordinating council or legislature may take different views,
but they would be dealing with definite alternatives. Most universities would prefer to make these choices internally; they
object to nonprofessionals making educational decisions, and
they deplore confounding educational decisions with politics.
Proponents of program budgeting might argue that properly
conceived decision packets permit determination of the level
of support of a unit or program without second-guessing the
professional judgment and competence of the staff or interfer-
ing with the internal budget. This is simply not true, and indicates naïveté. Quality is the issue which creates the conflict.
The difference between providing transportation by a Chevrolet
or a Cadillac is reasonably obvious. But in education the quality continuum is much more complicated. There is little agreement on educational quality or how to assure it. It is not clearly
related to a price tag. There is no precise correspondence between the support granted to a program and the quality of the
final product, and thus neither the planners nor the program
administrators can operate with complete autonomy.

THE ISSUE OF NONINTERFERENCE

In discussions of program budgeting it has been argued
that once the level of support has been decided, an operating
unit should be privileged to use savings from one part of its
program or task to initiate some other activity. Thus, there
would be no interference with internal operations. This is a

tempting prospect; it would provide an incentive for departments or colleges to seek more economical ways to operate programs if the savings could then be used to expand other programs or start new ones. But therein lies an inconsistency: A department which presented and was budgeted for the least expensive program alternatives would have no flexibility, while one which concealed less costly alternatives would acquire flexibility. Budget flexibility permitting retention of savings for alternative uses can result in commitments which require budgetary increases at the next round unless the alternatives are limited to nonrecurrent items such as equipment purchases or a limited research support.

Clearly, noninterference with internal operations once funds have been allocated admits that funding obtained on one basis can be used otherwise. Such use or misuse of funds is exactly what program budgeting seems designed to eliminate. Increasing class size and using teaching assistants to gain resources for research or graduate programs are the sorts of abuses that have led to demands for closer control. If there is no interference in one year with use of savings, there may have to be when the next budget request is made, or else program budeting is rendered ineffective by those who place their own priorities ahead of their accountability for funds.

MANAGEMENT INFORMATION SYSTEM NEEDED

Program budgeting, to be effective, must move from planning and analysis to budget development (which requires choices among the alternatives); and, with the use of a management information system which provides information feedback, it must provide for evaluating and auditing the performance as a basis for further planning. In particular, the audit must determine whether the fund allocated to a unit was used as originally projected. This requires much tighter management and control than universities presently find desirable; with present tools it is often not possible. One university official in a state requiring program budgeting remarked that expenditure coding and local personnel classification are not presently possible in its information system, and program budgeting cannot work until they are.

Many large institutions have tried to develop unified data systems which would enable them to tie together the university's operation and lead to wiser allocation of available space and resources. Such data systems are expensive and time-consuming to develop. There is, too, a general resistance to data collection, and those who do collect data must sort through manipulated data from most sources. What stance does one take with a professor who refuses to fill out a form (or does it facetiously) indicating how his hours are occupied? One can be reasonably sure that his associates will not censure him, nor will they condone punitive actions. Planning and program-budgeting systems that require such data can—if the data are reliable —help planners and administrators at all levels achieve insight into the internal operations of a university.

APPROACHES TO PROGRAM DEFINITION

The success of program budgeting ultimately depends not only on information systems but also upon finding program definitions acceptable and useful both to the universities and to those responsible for allocating funds. There are several approaches. In Michigan, the governor and the Bureau of Programs and Budget told universities that they must develop program budgets. All levels of education were listed as categories under a major program entitled Intellectual Development and Education. The category "higher education" was divided into twenty-one subcategories, including fifteen curriculum or career fields: business and commerce, health professions, biological and physical sciences, all other instructional fields requiring no more than five years of preparation, and six other subcategories: public service, research, financial aid to students, library services, student services, and administrative support. The subgoal statement for the program category "higher education" was defined as "to establish conditions whereby students are enabled to advance educationally beyond the secondary level in a manner consistent with their aspirations, abilities, and the presence of career opportunities."

After long and (from the university's point of view) fruitless discussions of appropriate programs and evidence of input and output, the Michigan budget office indicated that it would ask the universities to supply the following for each program: (1) ratio of (a) students receiving certification of achievement at each degree level from associate to doctorate to (b) the number of students finding career or advanced education placement at each level within six months after certification; (2) mean entry-level salary of students finding career placement at each degree level from associate to doctorate; and (3) percentage of students finding educationally related career placement at each degree level from associate to doctorate.

The ambiguity of the program subcategories makes one doubt the worth of this analysis either for budgeting or management. The attempted definition of input indicators and outputs was even more disconcerting. The three output measures indicate a lack of understanding of the realities of a large university. Questionnaires to determine career or educational placement (item 1) sent to graduates may achieve a 50 or 60 per cent return. By expenditure of excessive time and money this return can be increased, but to do this four times a year for all graduates would be unrealistic. Mean entry-level salary (item 2) poses similar difficulty and the additional problem that some persons do not respond to requests about salary or misrepresent it. Percentage of students finding *educationally related* career placement (item 3) is ambiguous. Again, it is a survey problem rather than a report of existing data.

Real concern attaches to the question of how such data would be used. The educator suspects that there need be no worry, for only "guesses" can be provided to such requests and no meaningful use for the results can be imagined. Yet one has a nagging suspicion that minds that could conjure up such specifications might also find some way to use them to the university's disadvantage. More sympathetically one might assume that under the pressures for PPBS, state officials with limited experience in such budgeting have hastily drawn up a format that complies with requirements but fails to accomplish the purpose.

THE OHIO MODEL

The Ohio Board of Regents (1971) has developed model program-expenditure budgets. The approach begins with a grouping of instructional programs into eight categories: general studies, technical education, baccalaureate general, baccalaureate professional, master's programs, graduate professional, doctor's programs, medical programs. The board considers five categories of work activity (instruction and general operations, research, public service, auxiliary services, and student aid) but develops the model program budget for only the first category. The procedures employed yield an estimated cost per thousand students for each of the eight categories of instructional programs. The model accomplishes three purposes: (1) establishing a level of state subsidy support for each type of program, (2) permitting equitable distribution of the state appropriations, (3) providing guidelines for institutional budgeting and expenditure. The model also permits a high degree of institutional flexibility. This fixed-budget approach encourages institutions to seek a combination of alternatives that produces the highest utility level for the given budget level. It can be contrasted with a program approach, which seeks to minimize costs by alternative modes of accomplishment.

THE APPROACH IN FLORIDA

In Florida (according to the program budget submitted to the governor of Florida by the Department of Administration, 1971), program budgeting breaks the major program of education into a number of subprograms; the division of universities appears in several subprograms but primarily in advanced and professional education (organized opportunities to pursue baccalaureate or advanced professional degrees). This subprogram is further divided into six elements: instruction, creative activity and research, public services, instructional and research support, student services, and state direction of advanced and professional education. Twenty-four subelements correspond to major curricular groupings. For each of these subelements, lower-division, upper-division, beginning-graduate, and advanced-graduate enrollments indicate the extent of the programs, and degrees awarded each year indicate the output. Costs are determined at this subelement level. Program budgeting thus corresponds closely to university organization and operations.

The efforts of the National Center for Higher Education Management Systems at Western Interstate Commission for Higher Education (1970) in developing its Program Classification Structure have resulted in a listing of three primary programs: instruction, research, and public service; and four supporting programs: academic support, student service, institutional service, and independent operations. Faculty activities, which might fall into any one of these seven programs, include teaching, student service, research and creative works, professional services, administration, other research and creative work, other professional service, and other activities. This definition of programs and activities more nearly approximates the concepts of programs and activities used on the campus. The definition can be applied across departments, colleges, institutes, and other university units. However, whether such program definitions will satisfy state budget officers and legislatures is somewhat uncertain.

One of the reasons given for the Michigan definition cited earlier was the necessity of reaching program definitions covering all levels and types of education. Universities are unlikely to use a program-budget request format exhibiting research as a separate item for review by legislators, who are notably unsympathetic to most types of academic research. Within the university the faculty will find the programs themselves somewhat arbitrary; the attempt to relate activities and programs will be resisted by many faculty members, receive perfunctory compliance by some, and be given needlessly conscientious and time-consuming introspection by others.

Unfortunately, this preoccupation with program definition may only serve to delay and reinforce administrators' hesitancy to make the unpopular decisions which they already know must be made. Whatever the program definitions, a budgetary and management information system must be devised which makes possible a more detailed analysis of needs and relates allocations to goals. There must also be auditing of data reported and evaluation of performance. Until this cycle is formulated and carried out expeditiously, program budgeting will be only a diversion.

COST-EFFECTIVENESS STUDIES

Demands for cost-effectiveness studies are closely related to program-budgeting procedures. The idea is that the cost of any particular program needs to be related to its effectiveness either in producing credit hours or degrees or in meeting social needs. Ultimately, budgetary officials would like to be able to predicate budgetary allocations upon the availability of such evidence. Universities generally distrust the comparability of such data because costing is in great part an artifact of the budget-allocation procedures used and depends a great deal on uniformity in definition of budget categories and on arbitrary decisions as to how expenditures for services and administration are folded back upon degree- or credit-producing units. Faculty time allocation to course instruction, advising, dissertation directing, and other functions is highly subjective and readily manipulated by departments or institutions. Moreover, departments which make extensive use of instructional services such as television, programmed learning materials, or computer-based instructions, which are budgeted elsewhere in the university, present difficult and as yet unsolved problems in cost determination.

Attempts to measure social or economic effectiveness in terms other than degrees or credits produced have not been successful and are, at best, projects for further research. Program-budgeting efforts which strive to include such evidence of effectiveness are simply unreasonable at this time.

State agencies have at times engaged in *preaudit,* a procedure whereby every requisition—whether for salaries, equipment, or travel—is reviewed to determine whether it is authorized by the budget and whether the indicated expenditure is reasonable. This procedure causes delay and threatens the efficient operation of institutional programs; it constitutes an almost intolerable limitation on autonomy and implies that the whole university staff is incapable of responsible behavior. The preaudit is expedited (and most obnoxious) when associated with a detailed line item budget which already denies flexibility in use of funds.

A PRESIDENT'S PLIGHT

Cheit (1971, p. 150) quotes at some length from a memorandum sent to him by a university president. The substance
of the memorandum (which could have been expressed by many
other presidents) is that precious little in the way of decision
making regarding expenditures is left to the campus. The gist
of the memorandum is as follows, concluded by a part of the
actual quotation: The state fund appropriation has sixteen
separate control appropriations. Constitutionally the governing
board has the power to shift funds, but the state insists that
funds forgone under any head be returned and vetoes any
unauthorized permanent augmentations of any individual appropriation. Thus, large-scale horizontal adjustments are pre-
cluded. Eliminating schools or colleges or departments and
diverting the released resources to other programs is possible
but not feasible. Since the state higher education plan requires
the university to accommodate the large numbers of students
assigned, eliminating one unit means transferring the students.
But only transfer of large numbers of students from high-cost
to low-cost areas would yield savings sufficient to achieve some
flexibility. Since budgeting on a multiyear basis is impossible,
"efficient" reallocations do not help the income-cost squeeze.
Tenure and other types of academic-personnel commitments
cannot readily be reduced in the short run. The attitudes surrounding the budget-making process place the president in a
bind.

> Faculty and students expect that the institution's bud-
> get requests will continue to express the real needs of the edu-
> cational program as they see them (that is, that they will seek
> to restore established standards of support, to sustain existing
> commitments, and to provide for incremental changes). . . .
> External budget-review agencies automatically start from the
> position that an institution's financial plan establishes the
> ceiling within which the annual budget review takes place.
> Thus, a public institution aiming to solve its income-cost
> problem by a long-range budget plan based on a realistic pre-
> diction of future state appropriations, in effect, is enunciating

a self-fulfilling prophecy. This is a course of action, moreover, which not only eliminates its chance (however small) to sustain the quality of its programs by eventually convincing the review agencies that it is in the state's interest to preserve educational standards; it also hazards appreciable internal disaffection and misunderstanding.

The situation is greatly complicated for institutions whose state legislatures appear to be hell-bent as a matter of policy on securing an overall increase in faculty "productivity" (input) irrespective of financial considerations. For such institutions, the development of budget plans based on what might seem to them to be realistic prognostications of future income is unlikely to head off this policy thrust thereby. Consequently, they invite a kind of a double jeopardy.

The frightful aspects of line item budgets and preaudit are implicit in this quotation. However, this particular institution seems to operate under a rigid form of these budgeting and control patterns.

FORMULA BUDGETING

Formula budgeting is not necessarily an alternative to program budgeting, since formulas can be applied to programs. By specifying for each department or course a section size and a faculty teaching load, institutions can determine their staffing requirements. Alternatively, staff needs may be estimated directly from projected numbers of students or student credit hours. Departmental support staff, supplies, services, and other support facilities can be determined by assigning a certain number of secretaries or technicians (and a certain number of dollars) for each specified block of faculty. Formulas for administrative staff in relation to institutional size and for libraries and other central services have been developed. Once an institutional appropriation has been determined by such means, the university may be permitted to budget internally without regard to the formula. Thus, the formula may appear to have limited internal impact. Nevertheless, rigid formulas damage institutional vitality because they take no account of quality. They are usually based on the operations for one or two years;

they may reflect a very inadequate budget allocation, but the formulas tend to perpetuate that pattern. This inflexibility does not accommodate changes in an institution's character or circumstances. When the formula is ignored internally, departments that do not get resources which they feel they have earned according to the formulas feel disadvantaged. When the formula is strictly applied, it presses institutions toward uniform mediocrity. The fact that the formula is regarded as having no validity for internal planning and budgeting raises doubts that it has validity for any other purpose.

Attempts to set up a system of planning and program budgeting (PPB) are direct incursions into the autonomy of institutions, because PPB enthusiasts insist that institutions prepare budgets and plans on patterns which many universities find irrelevant or even antithetical. But persons in institutions where PPB has been prescribed indicate that it has had essentially no effect on day-to-day operations. The lack of understanding of those who devise program-budget definitions irrelevant to the operation of the university is a factor; but developing program definitions applicable across a group of institutions, as well as devising the necessary transformations to move from budgeting to the operational level, may be insurmountable problems.

Nevertheless, program planning is a desirable alternative to the hand-to-mouth existence led by universities. And planning is virtually meaningless unless it is related to financial needs. The difficulty with present attempts at program planning and budgeting is that they are much too closely related to the immediate budget negotiations and are pushed or enforced by budget offices and legislative committees, which (whatever they say) are little inclined to look beyond next year's budget requests and available resources. When a strong coordinating board charged with institutional role determination and state planning for higher education undertakes this PPBS approach on a consistent and continuing basis, significant results can be achieved. Long-term planning requires time and expertise; it cannot be left to persons already overloaded by the demands of current budget review and processing.

ULTIMATELY—POLITICS

A university's projection of "needs" (institutional or social), whether in a program budget or otherwise, is only one input into a collective, highly complex, and sometimes very messy political process. Projections of needs for professionals and technicians in various fields are subject to error. Cost-benefit and cost-effectiveness analysis, despite the glowing words about them, are inexact. The benefits of an education have never yet been and are not likely to be soon appraised in a manner widely acceptable to educators, economists, politicians, and the citizens generally.

The ultimate decisions about the budgets of state universities are ultimately political, whether one focuses on the executive office or the legislature. Legislative committees, state and national, may seek to establish priorities and seek expert advice in so doing. They also receive "expert" advice in quantity by special interests—sources which are frequently contradictory. The politician must also be sensitive to public reactions. If the public does not think that the university is producing benefits the public will not support increased taxes and may not reelect the legislators who levy them. Both the university and the legislature look to the future: the university views the appropriation in reference to its plans and aspirations, while the legislator views appropriations in reference to his own future. Also, the legislator may have in his own district a state college or university which directly and indirectly pressures for increase in funds and programs.

The public may not understand the issues involved in university budgets, but its collective view about the university's irresponsibility and about increasing costs can crystallize an issue. The legislator, sensitive to this fact, may be forced to find a rationale for giving the university less than requested. Budgetary items which can be ridiculed, incidents on campus which can be cited as evidence of radicalism or lack of control, even personal animosities can in this circumstance become the basis (either overt or covert) for arbitrary reductions in budgets. Small wonder it is that administrators wince at presenting program details before legislators, knowing that this may be their own undoing when the budget officer or legislators are primarily seeking justification for a budget cut that they have already decided to make.

State budget officers make their reputations largely by their effectiveness in reducing requests for funds. They expect padding and continually devise ways of detecting and eliminating it. Year after year budget offices seek for the crucial data that will reveal the truth about "real" needs. The university responds (if at all) with estimates, and the inaccuracies and inconsistencies are all too apparent. Before the university can gear up its data-collection procedures to supply accurately what is requested, the data request may be changed.

Many higher education administrations are not convinced that legislators or budget officers will persist in attempts to reform higher education. They even doubt that compliance or noncompliance with data requests and budgetary formats makes any difference in the size of the institutional and total higher edcation appropriation. Some educators view present demands and criticism as an irritation, assuming that—like past episodes of this type—this, too, will pass. Unfortunately, they may be right. We hope not. More effective use of resources is needed. University priorities need revision. Planning and program budgeting can provide a better basis for management; but management will improve only if administrators, buttressed by more incisive information and clearer goals than at present, will make the decisions indicated.

8

Coordinating Boards and State Systems

A degree of coordination for the state-supported institutions of higher education has always existed. Where no other agency has existed, the legislature itself has provided some coordination through the budgetary process. In some cases other executive agencies, even state purchasing agencies, have provided a degree of coordination.

Coordination is a way to attain efficiency and economy in state educational enterprises when the following goals are met: (1) adequate diversity in educational programs and a reasonable measure of institutional distinctiveness; (2) designation and maintenance of institutions' functions that contribute to their distinctiveness; (3) comprehensive educational planning, which covers expansion of some institutions, erection of additional institutions, and specification of the character and location of each; (4) control necessary to avoid duplication in programs; (5) mediation between institutions and state government in resource allocation.

State coordinating boards and their staffs differ from university system boards and their staffs in role and patterns of organization, but from our point of view they pose much the same issues with regard to autonomy. State coordinating boards, which are involved in university budgets and work with state offices and legislatures in obtaining appropriations, naturally become deeply concerned with the justification of institutional requests. For successful operation, a coordinating board must be seen by state officials and the legislature as a control over universities, while seen by universities as supportive of their aspirations for funds and programs. Should either side be completely happy with the coordinating group, it is almost certain that the other will be equally unhappy and that the board may shortly become ineffective.

In dealing with planning and budgeting, any centralized board or staff has some advantages of overview, remoteness, and objectivity. But these same advantages can be viewed by both institutions and by the legislature as disadvantages. Each may feel that the board is not sufficiently familiar with the campus to understand or adequately represent its needs. The institution wants more money; the legislature wants more efficiency. Coordinating groups quickly find that they are unable to react critically to institutional requests without hard data, but data supplied by the institutions are neither comparable nor adequate and may reflect a carefully calculated institutional bias. Hence, one of the first needs of any central office coordinating several campuses is to develop a data system and techniques for defining and collecting elements in standard and verifiable form. The normal tendency is to push toward system uniformity. This will be resisted by any institutions in the system that have already achieved a major reputation as high-quality institutions and are therefore likely to have higher salaries and higher costs than other institutions. Weaker or developing institutions in the system are likely to welcome uniformity in salaries and support levels. This uniformity may doom all of the institutions in a system to the same dull mediocrity.

Coordinating or control boards inevitably move toward (1) designation of institutional and departmental roles to avoid unnecessary duplication within a state, (2) approval of new programs and degrees to ensure that they are actually needed and that funds are available for their support, (3) development of an appropriations formula based upon instructional load, and (4) both position and salary control. The result approaches a line item budget, which is highly inflexible (although perhaps a procedural rather than substantive restriction) and strikes at the autonomy of a campus and at the departments therein.

If a state coordinating board can successfully develop procedures regarded as fair by the institutions, it may be able to collapse institutional budget requests into a single figure; the board can then present this figure to the legislature, indicating how requests were derived rather than exhibiting detailed figures for particular institutions. If this can be done, the board will effectively screen the institutions from a variety of political pressures commonly brought to bear in negotiating institutional budget requests. Nevertheless, a coordinating board's activities do filter through university autonomy to impact upon unit operations. Without looking at the plans and programs of each individual unit, the board has very little recourse except to approve the total university proposal. Generally speaking, the staff of a coordinating board will be in closer touch with the academic world and somewhat more difficult to deceive than the typical state budget officer or legislator. Thus, an institution may find its program proposals subjected to a closer scrutiny and its later actions viewed by a more insightful eye.

LEVELS OF COORDINATION

Four levels of coordination or control can be identified. The first level is voluntary cooperation, seen in organizations such as the Michigan Council of State College Presidents. This council discusses common problems of state institutions in Michigan and occasionally commissions studies that have had a significant impact on the institutions, but it has largely avoided budgetary matters. In Indiana, where for many years only four institutions were involved, voluntary cooperation in developing a composite budget request has proved very effective. (Both Michigan and Indiana now have a form of state-wide coordination.) On the whole, however, voluntary cooperation has been ineffective, since institutions cooperate only when it is to their advantage. One might suspect that some cooperative agencies have served chiefly as a façade to beguile legislatures and the public into feeling that effective cooperation among institutions already exists.

On the second level, boards or commissions coordinate several or all state institutions, exercising differing functions depending upon the legislation which brought them into being; usually they are concerned with planning new programs and developing a composite budget request. On the third level a stronger means of coordination is achieved by consolidating several institutions into a single university. A well-known example is the University of North Carolina, which includes North Carolina State College at Raleigh, the Woman's College at Greensboro, and also the Chapel Hill campus of the University of North Carolina; each institution has its own chancellor, but all are part of a consolidated system with a president and a common board of trustees. Consolidated state universities also exist in California, New York, Wisconsin, and elsewhere. (Recently both North Carolina and Wisconsin have brought all state universities and colleges under a single board.)

The meaning of consolidation is not always clear. The physical decentralization of higher education in every state makes control of each campus difficult. The typical pattern (under consolidation) of a chief executive on each campus, each with its own board, suggests that individual campuses have retained some initiative, and the mere incorporation of several institutions under a single name does not change that fact. On the other hand, the existence of a central office with an executive and a full-time staff monitoring the activities of several campuses may markedly limit local autonomy by control of programs, determination of priorities, and appointment of the chancellor. A step beyond coordination is that of central control; that is, a central governing board has authority, corresponding to that usually held by a single institutional board, over several institutions. Consolidation may yield a central governing board, but within a given state there may be a consolidation of several different groups of institutions into single composite institutions without providing a central governing board over all. Finally, on the fourth level are master boards with supervisory powers over the usual institutional governing boards.

Berdahl (1971), in his study of state coordination, reports, as of 1969, only two states with no formal coordination. Forty-one of the state coordinating agencies had jurisdiction over all or almost all of public higher education, and several were attempting to include private institutions in their planning. Berdahl's study reveals a trend toward stronger coordination and control in recent years.

REASONS FOR COORDINATION

The reason why states insist upon more coordination and control is obvious. More and more students have enrolled in public education, a trend that will probably continue. As a result, the publicly supported institutions have been demanding more funds for operating and for expanding facilities. New institutions and campuses have had to be planned, and existing institutions have had to be given increased support.

Many small institutions have sought to grow larger, to become more like a major state university. They have sometimes been led by administrative officers who wanted to build their own empires. In these expansionist pressures one can find some major arguments against coordination: it stifles the initiative of institutions, creates excessive standardization, and breeds mediocrity. A common argument is that competitive autonomy produces more diversity and better quality than coordination. There is just enough truth in this argument to give the appearance of reasonableness. The actual fact is that competitive autonomy has led to uniformity and standardization.

As states have developed more institutions, a recognized division of labor has frequently developed, which institutions hesitate to accept. State universities with professional and graduate programs are becoming increasingly oriented to the needs of junior and senior transfer students. State colleges and city colleges, formerly devoted chiefly to preparing teachers and undergraduate professional specialties, have increasingly presumed to become nationally and internationally known universities with a broad range of programs and a graduate school. One might expect two-year and four-year regional institutions and community colleges to concentrate on two-year programs and vocational programs that do not require further study; in fact, however, four-year institutions seldom want to offer only the first two years of any program. Community colleges, to a greater extent than is desirable, seem to focus on programs preparatory for transfer; even supposedly terminal programs often involve expectations that students may wish to earn a B.A. degree. Hence, too many community colleges design most of their programs to be acceptable for transfer. Finally, universities—which are expected to concentrate on junior, senior, and graduate professional programs—usually insist on maintaining large freshman and sophomore programs; they can teach such programs economically, by using graduate students as teachers, and thereby obtain both funds and students for their graduate programs. But the research-oriented university departments are not satisfactory units for handling the first two years of college.

The definition of institutional roles, achievement of efficiency, and rationalization of educational planning will be achieved only by limiting the autonomy of individual institutions. Loose coordination may be effective when resources are easily obtained and the main concern may be to ward off unnecessary duplication of new programs. When resources are tighter, a coordinating council needs a more rigorous point of view.

INSTITUTIONAL ROLE ASSIGNMENT

To determine the role of an institution, it is necessary to have a plan for the state or region, taking into account total resources and educational needs. Each institution should have a range of programs and degrees (baccalaureate, master's, or doctoral) which it is permitted to offer. Such role definition will call for some cooperation between state and federal government in order to avoid federal funding of institutional aspirations that have, at times, been inconsistent with state plans. Major institutional grants from foundations or from government agencies should be screened and approved by coordinating agencies to determine that developments supported by these grants are needed and are consistent with institutional roles. Only by such review is it possible to ensure that the acceptance of such grants does not ultimately require additional unscheduled state support.

Role assignment also permits universities to limit their services to an appropriate clientele. The argument that any state-supported university should be open to all comers lacks logical or legal grounds. The state provides many kinds of services (prisons, hospitals, schools, workmen's compensation), each of which is limited to individuals who meet certain requirements. To give every person opportunity to pursue education insofar as he can profit from it is not the same as assuring him admission to any educational institution he wishes to attend. The institutional role should permit selectivity in admissions as well as in programs.

It sometimes seems that the main concern of coordinating boards is to collect a great mass of data and (mis)use it in some mysterious way to generate a composite budget request, but actually the first and major function of a coordinating board is to develop and maintain a state plan for higher education. Individual institutions cannot make such a plan for themselves, particularly when cutbacks are required. Even if each institution produces a plan, a collection of egocentric institutional plans does not add up to a state plan. A complete state educational plan should take into account the definition of roles for both private and public institutions. It makes no sense to add expensive new programs (especially graduate and professional) to public institutions when existing programs in private institutions could meet the need. The acceptance of state or federal dollars by private institutions surely obligates them to accept also the combination of private and public institutions as a single system. The plan should consider what type of postsecondary education is required to serve young persons who will be attending college as well as adults seeking more education. Society's need for various types of education in various locales must be considered. As prospective needs become apparent, resources found in existing institutions must be reviewed.

The planners must ask: To what extent can these institutions be expanded, either on the present campuses or through branches, to take care of these needs? Should the character or scope of programs at some institutions be narrowed or broadened? What institutions should be added? Where? How will they relate to existing institutions? Should some programs be duplicated? Questions about admissions, tuition fees, credit transferability, and enrollment mixes or ceilings are essential parts of any state plan.

Specific attention must be given to graduate professional programs and graduate programs. These have high prestige, which spurs the tendency of four-year institutions to want to move into the next level of education. The research and public-service programs available in the institutions, and the relationship of these programs to state needs, must also be carefully studied—in particular, the question of whether existing institutions can meet certain social problems or whether new centers or institutes are needed. As one thinks of the total system of higher education, it becomes increasingly important to consider computer facilities, library facilities, instructional television and other expensive instructional equipment, and educational technology generally, as possibilities for cooperation among institutions to improve education and to use scarce resources more efficiently. Computer and instructional television units may require direct coordination and control at the state level to ensure that these facilities are equally available to all institutions and that some commonly agreed-upon set of priorities can be applied in determining access to the equipment.

The duplication of resources in extension courses demands coordination. Partly because of limitation on transfer of credits from one institution to another, partly because universities feel that offering courses at a distance broadens their political support, faculty members from different institutions may travel major distances to offer courses duplicated in other extension locales by other institutions. This situation can be resolved only at the state level. It probably requires a central extension program to handle requests for service, survey needs and resources, assist institutions in programing, and set geographical boundaries.

One major element in planning is to examine the availability of needed resources for the next ten, fifteen, or twenty-five years. Although one cannot foresee all contingencies, it should be possible to project estimated tax revenues and to consider whether these in relationship to other demands for state services are likely to allow sufficient funds for all the recommendations. One problem is that all projections are only refinements of population forecasts; estimated tax revenues, demands for state services, and needs for education all flow from the same source. The trick is to chart the rocks and shoals that can create rapids and backwaters. There is little point in putting out a state plan which is completely unrealistic in terms of available resources. On the one hand, undue optimism is created in the institutions and in the regions of the state that may get new institutions; on the other hand, the legislature and others involved in providing the funds are likely to become disenchanted with the whole plan.

A difficult task is the elimination of unneeded duplicate programs. Teacher education offered in almost all institutions may be justified, but duplicate programs in fields such as forestry, engineering, and agriculture probably are not. A particular regional industry or natural resource may justify a special program in engineering or agriculture, even though the major program is elsewhere. Cooperation among institutions could enrich individual experiences through dual registration, exchange of students or faculty, or use of communication devices.

Degree-credit requirements, credits assigned to particular courses, and the level at which courses are placed are other sources of unnecessary expense. If one campus requires 180 quarter credits for a degree while another requires 200, degrees

will tend to cost more in the latter institution while not necessarily being of superior quality. Credits assigned to courses may
have little relationship to the work required. The level of a
course affects those budgets based upon differential support by
level, but examples of introductory freshman-level courses
offered at the upper-class or graduate level can be found in
many universities.

LIMITING FACULTY SALARIES AND RANKS

Salaries account for a high percentage of the budgets,
and the variations in salary levels among institutions suggest
that salary controls can lead simultaneously to uniformity and
economy. Uniformity in salaries leaves no room for merit recognition and reduces the incentive for the individual faculty
member. Since institutional quality varies greatly, salaries
should not be dictated uniformly over a system; but the importance of salaries will ultimately lead to some external constraints. Under collective bargaining, it is predictable that a
high degree of uniformity in salary patterns will emerge.

Closely related to faculty salary is the matter of distribution by rank and the percentage of faculty on tenure. Limiting
the percentage in the top two ranks to 50 per cent is appropriate
to ensure a faculty's continued ability to adjust to change and
to guard against artificially increasing costs. Retirements and
resignations provide some flexibility, but it has often been lost
by allowing units to retain vacancies and refill them at the same
or higher level. A policy that all replacements must be at the
lowest rank would achieve some economies but ignore justifiable exigencies. Imposition of such policies by a coordinating
board could mean that institutional budgets would be inflexibly
gauged to this practice. A policy with considerable leeway in
application would be better.

Limitation on the percentage of the faculty granted
tenure is desirable. We are not impressed with the argument
that tenure is essential to academic freedom. Our immediate
concern is that the practice of rapid promotions in recent years,
coupled with early granting of tenure, has contributed to inflexibility in use of resources and to the deterioration in faculty

quality. The imposition of a minimum age for the granting of tenure, perhaps forty-five, with the further provision that no one joining the staff of an institution prior to age forty could receive tenure for at least ten years, would be a desirable measure to counterweight present tenure practices. Another possibility is a series of five-year contracts up to fifty-five and then a terminal ten-year contract.

Other items involving faculty have become matters of public concern: extensive travel, absence from the classroom without prior announcement or replacement, negligence in keeping office hours, and excessive consulting for fees. Many universities have statements of policy on these matters, but administrators are handicapped in either collecting information or enforcing policy because of faculty stance. What the individual campus does not do must be externally forced; again, this should be done by general policy statements rather than by review of individual cases.

Classroom and student-station utilization is poor on most campuses. Station-utilization percentages will never approach 100 per cent, but there is little excuse for low percentages—40 to 60 per cent—in the utilization of rooms during a forty- or forty-four-hour week. Primarily, the problem is that faculty and students reject late-afternoon classes. A principle should be defined at the state level and strongly enforced to require that uniform space-utilization data be gathered regularly and consulted whenever universities request new facilities.

NEED FOR EVIDENCE

Planning is always a continuing function because needs change as interest and motivation within higher education change and the availability of resources changes. A plan must be continually monitored in reference to reality as reality replaces imagination. This activity increases demands for uniform data gathering and accounting procedures to estimate costs. Concerns about costs lead to questions about courses and about student and faculty loads. Answers require definitions of terms such as course level, student level, and full-time enrollment. To provide more objectivity in making decisions and to avoid political battles, formulas may be developed for such areas as student-faculty ratios, salary level by ranks, space requirements, and admission quotas.

A system such as we have talked about eventually requires evidence which relates effectiveness of individual institutions to their resource utilization. No coordinating group or governing board has yet moved to this stage, simply because faculty members have never been able to agree on the outcomes of their courses; those who debate the economic and social benefits of higher education are no closer to agreement now than they were a quarter of a century ago.

Research on instructional patterns provides no clear guidelines. Some researchers assert that discussion groups and smaller classes are more effective in promoting affective outcomes, but few faculty members are really concerned with such outcomes. The matter is largely one of faculty and student preference rather than of educational quality. Resources should be available to support justified variations—for example, in teaching the educationally disadvantaged; but tradition or preference for small class sizes is not a sufficient basis for budget allocation. Ultimately, class size and teaching load may be decided by collective bargaining, and then neither the local campus nor the state coordinating council will have much impact. Meanwhile, a coordinating council should provide general injunctions for instructional patterns and request justification for atypical and expensive patterns.

Though the citizens and the legislature may feel that the existence of a coordinating or control board assures more effective use of resources, it is not obvious that this is so. There are no criteria available on educational quality. Educational costs within a state may vary with the cost of living from one section of the state to another. There is, as yet, no way to figure the return on an educational investment. The credit hours or the number of degrees produced can be used for figuring costs, but it tells us nothing about the program's actual benefits to the individual or the community. Demands for study and evaluation will continue; and if anything is accomplished, it will likely be from a coordinating effort external to institutions and separated from budget officials and the legislature.

COORDINATING RESPONSES TO SOCIAL PROBLEMS

Many new social problems and challenges seem beyond the reach of universities. Faculty members and administrators often lack the experience and interest to attack such social problems as health, ecology, and the inner-city ghetto. If they do attempt to confront the problems, institutions almost invariably operate as single autonomous units, but institutions acting individually cannot meet the demands of the day. Their organization is cumbersome, and each institution is often decentralized to the point where it cannot manage effective collaboration with others and cannot achieve a larger view of a system in which it is only a part. Moreover, universities are seldom budgeted for new research and service activities. Their inadequate plans and their competition for support funds necessitate coordination and planning at the state, regional, or even national level. The staff of the several state institutions may, at times, have to be regarded as a composite resource to be reallocated to meet changing demands or to use changing faculty competencies. Private research institutions; clearinghouses on facilities, programs, resources, and personnel; consortia; state institutes—all are needed to provide better ways to meet social problems, new or old.

When a governing board defines success in terms of meeting social needs, university faculties and administrators will know that the ultimate invasion of their autonomy has come about. Rather than being responsible for preparing students to fulfill certain roles in society and for providing courses and programs the universities conceive as relevant, they would find their decisions about academic affairs scrutinized by an outside group. This has already been done in many cases by professional accrediting associations, which have looked primarily at the process rather than the outcome. In England within the last year, the output of some of the theoretical engineering programs was not considered relevant to industry;

consequently, the support for these programs was shifted to programs considered more practical. When this occurs, it must be obvious to the faculty that the university no longer has the privilege of defining the professionally trained person.

CONSOLIDATED UNIVERSITY SYSTEMS

The move to coordination or to consolidated university systems was given some support when universities proved unable to meet local educational needs even by establishing branches. For example, the University of Wisconsin two-year branches (now absorbed into the university system) were effectively dominated by the Madison faculty and run essentially as "farm clubs," with junior faculty and with strict limitations on the courses offered. A similar pattern existed in Ohio, where a number of the universities operated various extension centers; the programs in these centers were fully determined by the home campus, and individuals were assigned to carry out instructional duties in a routine manner. Such operations caused no threat to the main campus (indeed, they were erroneously viewed as feeders) because they were controlled from the home base and they often provided a source of additional funds. In some cases, a very sizable percentage of money allocated by the legislature to the operation of a branch campus was peeled off for "administrative costs" on the major campus before being made available to the regional extension center. Under such domination and exploitation, these branches have proved unsatisfactory to local communities and branch staffs alike.

A university system, with its board and staff, has impacts upon a particular campus in much the same way as a state coordinating board does, but there are some significant differences. In the past, when such a system was created by combining several campuses, the president of the major university campus frequently became the president of the system. Such a president found it difficult (or simply refused) to separate himself from the operation of the campus over which he formerly presided. In such a pattern he maintained his earlier role and used his expanded office to protect that campus against expansion by others. This situation became particularly exasperating for other campuses that had been made full units of the new system, for they considered themselves as equal though not yet full partners with the original campus and expected to be supported at the same level. For example, the Milwaukee, Parkside, and Green Bay campuses of the University of Wisconsin consider themselves equal to the Madison campus, while some persons at the Madison campus expect the university system to preserve Madison's primacy. Unequal treatment often encourages subsidiary campuses to push for an independent status; and given the right kinds of political pressures, they may achieve it. When it happens, it does so because branch roles were not clearly specified and aspirations of branches were not being met.

The farther away a branch is from the main campus, the less the possibility of intervention into its operational details. Intercampus faculty senates or committees are time-consuming and costly. Regular visits to each branch by central university administrators would seem to be a good means of communication and coordination. However, reactions of those doing so are mixed. Just being "available" may turn out to be a waste of time; actively meeting with committees and individuals may be perceived as unjustified interference. The chief executive officer of a university system should have campus administrative and faculty experience, but he probably should be officed in the state capital and limit his campus visits to occasional "inspections" and discussions of major local problems and problems which he can relate to the total system.

SOME COMPLICATIONS IN CONSOLIDATION

Our studies of particular university systems presented several instances of serious problems: (1) The chief executive officer of a branch campus was overshadowed when the chief executive officer of the whole university system was also on that campus. (2) The president of the university system viewed the other campuses of the university as relatively minor parts of his concern. (3) The board of the consolidated university, when it had previously been the board for the major campus and had retained many of its members, gave more attention to the main campus and less to other branches. (4) The prerogatives retained by consolidated university executives varied greatly: in one case the campus chief executive was disturbed because the president of the consolidated university retained control of the executive football box, although the football stadium was on that campus. In another case the consolidated university president retained the right—according to bylaws—to preside over the meetings on each of the several campuses. In still another case the president insisted that every new prospective appointee for a position of associate or full professor should be brought to his office for interview. In another case, our request for interviews on a campus created some consternation because it was addressed to the campus executive rather than to the university executive. We learned that all correspondence requesting the university's cooperation on any project must be directed to the university president rather than to a campus chancellor.

These instances are meant to point up the fact that consolidated university systems often face problems because one or two institutions in the consolidation have the major prestige, or perhaps one of them has been the "real" university while the branch campuses were extension centers. When the system employs administrators who had been on the major campus and whose offices remain there, real difficulties are in prospect. We would suggest that the president of any composite university system have an office elsewhere than on any one of the campuses and that, generally speaking, it is unwise to attempt to transform the chief executive of the major campus into the chief executive for the university.

SHORTCOMINGS OF COORDINATION

Thus far, state coordinating boards leave much to be desired. On one hand, as in Florida, so much of the board's time seems to be involved in negotiating with various state offices and the legislature that some of the serious problems of coordination among institutions are left untouched. In Florida and several other states, the delineation of roles for various institutions has not been sufficiently clear; political considerations have often defeated a board's attempts to prescribe institutional roles and to provide educational opportunity on an effective and efficient basis to all segments of the state. In Illinois, the recent Phase III report of the state plan indicates an intent to review all duplicative programs, strengthen role definitions, relate state plans to private higher education, and introduce research and service institutes to coordinate the efforts of all universities. In the face of constricted funds the Illinois board has also requested institutions to develop a list outlining the order in which programs would be eliminated to achieve 15 per cent reduction in the operating budget. (Memorandum to Chief Academic and Program Officers of Illinois Public Colleges and Universities and Systems from Steven B. Sample, Deputy Director for Programs, Board of Higher Education, September 8, 1971.)

North Carolina recently created a powerful new governing board for higher education. This state, like many others, has faced a long period of bitter competition for appropriations between the University of North Carolina with its multiple campuses and the ambitious former state teachers' colleges. The new board, approved by the legislature on recommendation of the governor, will have broad powers over all sixteen of the public four-year and graduate institutions, including approval of new programs, elimination of unproductive or unnecessary old ones, determination of priorities, and designation of the campus chancellors. In Wisconsin a recent action brought together all of the state institutions in a somewhat similar pattern. In April 1971, the Indiana legislature created a statewide coordinating agency, bringing to forty-seven the number of states with such agencies (Education Commission of the States, 1971). Most coordinating commissions or control boards responsible for several campuses are hesitant about reallocating functions or programs from one institution to another. Specific direction by the legislature is helpful, since it allows control boards to point out that they are forced to take certain actions by the legislature.

An area for which coordination often has failed is that of new programs. For a number of years, for example, the Illinois State Board of Higher Education continued to review all new programs for approval or denial. Approval meant that the budget proposed for that institution usually included additional money for the cost of that program. But once a program had been approved by the board, the institution was privileged to go ahead with it whether or not additional funds were made available. Recently the Illinois board has apparently taken the point of view that new programs will not be permitted to start unless new resources are provided.

Coordinating boards for state systems of higher education have had difficulty deciding what to do about private education and programs in state institutions supported by nonstate funds. With regard to the latter, any program started in a state institution should be cleared with a coordinating board, which can examine long-term budget implications and then decide whether the program is really needed, whether it competes with other programs in the state, and so on. Attempts to plan and control program development are useless if institutions, on the basis of a small amount of money for a year or two, can get by with initiating programs that have not been approved. In the private sector the problem is more complicated. Undoubtedly many existing programs in private institutions could be subsidized by the state at lower cost than would be necessary to add them to existing programs in public institutions. At the same time, private institutions must realize that accepting subsidies for educational programs brings them within the orbit of the state coordinating or controlling group. They can expect to be asked for certain statistics and to have their costs and efficiency considered in much the same way as fully state-supported institutions.

Institutional self-interest impedes effective coordination in many ways. State universities as well as private colleges and universities, as a matter of self-preservation, lobby against creating new colleges in a state. They would apparently rather expand their own programs or even let a few individuals be denied educational opportunities than to see resources diverted into new programs. New programs are always a source of competition among institutions. Professional schools—law, medicine, dentistry, and others—have such prestige that universities often compete for them, although the severe financial demands may be cause later for regret. Even the fact that an institution in the state is considering the development of a four-year degree program in, let us say, cosmetology will almost certainly generate action on a number of other campuses. The reasons are manifold: (1) Some publicity always attaches to a new program. (2) Some hope always arises that a new program will result in a new fund source. (3) An institution that regularly adds programs is believed to be dynamic and therefore worthy of support for other innovative activity. (4) Some faculty members are always seeking a chance to advance themselves regardless of the field. Such persons are likely to seize an opportunity to develop a new program, hoping that they may acquire the title of director or dean. Local pride also is a factor, although pride in a local institution of higher education has diminished somewhat in recent years. In times past local people frequently hoped that new programs would attract more people and resources to the community.

Another impediment to coordination is the legislature itself. Some legislators with attachments to particular institutions form blocs that can effectively prevent a coordinating board from enforcing unpopular though necessary decisions, especially in eliminating unneeded programs. What is frequently demonstrated when the planning and coordination of higher education move to a more central and visible role is just how political many educational decisions are. Those well acquainted with the university campus have always known this and are not surprised to find the same political interests also operating in the broader state-level arena.

Institutions fear, perhaps rightly, that coordination will add another echelon of authority with more red tape and costs but no advantages. But if coordinating boards determine institutional roles and hold institutions to them, the fully developed universities and the public will clearly gain. Boards must present strong cases and gain respect and support from the public, the governor's office, and the institutions. To do this, coordination will have to move from a focus on input to output accountability. Output accountability poses several difficult, perhaps unsolvable problems; input characterization requires definition

in terms of common external criteria. Until both input and
output can be described and measured according to external
criteria, they cannot be validly related in ways that justify internal control of institutions by an external agency. Qualitative
evaluation by public agencies (perhaps a reinterpretation and
extension of current accrediting procedures) might prove more
satisfactory than any quantitative method conceived at present.
But the difficulties of such evaluation (as well as faculty and
administration aversion to it) cast doubt on any attempts to
base coordination and budgeting entirely on external criteria.
Accordingly, coordination is likely to require much internal
probing of institutions and continuing attempts to develop uniform data collection.

COORDINATION IN BRITAIN

The problem of coordination is not unique to the United
States. In Great Britain the universities are independent, self-
governing institutions established by charter. Accordingly, like
universities with constitutional status in this country, they are
free to conduct their own affairs without parliamentary control
or ministerial directive. Nevertheless, like American universities, they depend largely for their funds on the state, and they
have major roles in the development of national policy. The
University Grants Committee provides the intermediate ma-
chinery by which public funds flow to the universities without
direct governmental intervention and in a manner consistent
with the maintenance of proper academic freedom and university autonomy.

The University Grants Committee is concerned with
planning the size and balance of universities in terms of student
numbers and resources. The UGC is responsible for developing a total plan for the country; and this plan, to be effective,
must include not only the whole higher education establishment but also the development of each university within that
whole. The making of grants, then, requires an extensive collection and analysis of the wide range of statistics. Some picture
of the general development of the institution over the next
quinquennium for which a grant will be made is essential. In-

stitutions may develop proposals for additional programs, but these must be screened in terms of the aspirations of other institutions, social needs, and the money available. Although each university ultimately attains a block grant, which it can use as it wishes, both the UGC and the government are looking more closely into the operation of individual institutions. Because of pressure from the Department of Education and Science, the UGC has become more explicit about the intended use of funds. The UGC has become concerned with faculty load, space utilization, distribution of the faculty across ranks; it is conducting cost studies and employing them to reduce the range of costs in specified fields. The UGC recently announced that not more than 35 per cent of the members of the academic staff could hold appointments at the top two ranks. Much of this intervention is conducted quietly, hidden from the public gaze; and perhaps much of it is successful because the several committees of the UGC are themselves heavily made up of administrators and faculty from the universities. At the moment British universities are under less restraint than some in this country, but considerably more than some others here. The indications there are that the intervention will increase, just as there is every reason to believe that the same thing will happen here.

At various points in the preceding discussion we have suggested specific means of control. It is appropriate to bring these together and point out that a coordinating board's general cautions and injunctions can be backed up by specific allocations of resources and roles. (1) A state plan will generally assign a role to each institution and specify the programs which that institution is authorized to operate. The plan may go so far as to indicate a maximum and minimum number of students necessary for the operation of the program: the minimum, to assure that the program does not compete with others in the state unless there is significant student demand; the maximum, to avoid one institution's seeking to attract students from the same programs offered elsewhere in the state or to ensure that an expensive program is not unduly expanded. (2) By defining the information required from institutions and setting up auditable procedures for the collection of that information, a coordinating board can reinforce its prerogatives of budget determination and resource allocation. If the data are accurate and irrefutable, the legislature and executive offices will come to look to the coordinating board for information on the institutions rather than to rely upon materials from the separate institutions. (3) By controlling the addition of new programs and their location and by continually reviewing existing programs, central boards can control the aspirations and operations of institutions and defend this control in terms of social needs and operational efficiency. (4) A coordinating board may undertake to assign productivity levels by campuses, taking into account the differences in the roles of campuses and the range of functions they pursue. Attempts to determine productivity levels will also be closely related to determination of section and class size and even to instructional models. (5) Control of the faculty rank distribution and the percentage of tenured faculty may be necessary in centralized coordination of institutions. When a large percentage of the faculty members of an institution hold the top ranks, costs are high because of high salaries and because of the smaller numbers of credits and students taught. The percentage of faculty holding tenure has a great effect on how flexible a campus can be in adjusting to change. (6) Standards for assigning new facilities and utilizing existing space may be useful in setting priorities among the continuing demands of separate campuses. (7) Centralized control or possibly a geographical pattern to control extension programs may be necessary to improve educational services while maintaining efficiency. (8) It may become necessary to set up, on a state-wide basis, a number of institutes or centers reporting directly to a coordinating board and to budget these directly but to staff them at least in part with faculty members selected for special competencies from the campuses.

As one examines these alternatives, each one of which has some sound rationale, one can see that the assessment of educational needs in the state and concern for their management can move very rapidly toward operational control. How one views this movement depends to a great extent upon his point of view and the range of considerations that he is willing to take into account. The importance and expense of the public university assure that the public is going to be concerned about its management. The faculty and administrators on a particular campus, if they were willing to operate in full awareness of this concern and the responsibilities involved, might be able to serve the public interest while operating with a high degree of autonomy. Whether they really could operate that way is doubtful, because inevitably they would face demands to establish the best possible university; and, unfortunately, they seldom define "best" as "that which promotes society's needs." Thus, continuing tension is inevitable between those who wish to forward the prestige of their university and those who demand greater sensitivity to social needs.

CONCLUSIONS

Higher education should be planned at the state, regional, and national levels. Basically, planning must take into account the allocation of resources in relationship to social needs and institutional roles.

A system of management information—which can be used to determine how resources are spent and what results are obtained—must be developed, defined at a central level, and so defined that it is verifiable.

There must be complete control over the addition of any new programs in state institutions. This means documentation of need and careful review of resources, staff, and facilities before a program is approved. Approval of a new program should be made contingent upon additional resources being allocated to develop that program.

The state coordinating agency should be charged with review and elimination of duplicative programs across a number of institutions. Recommendations for elimination of duplicative programs should be supported by budget action.

State-wide productivity levels must be specified on a basis that can be audited but permits necessary adaptations on each campus.

The number of faculty at higher rank and on tenure should be controlled.

A plan for utilization of private institutions is essential

to avoid duplication of programs. Provision of educational services should be viewed in terms of the total cost to the individual and the state, and education should be available to all
citizens at equal cost (unless one deliberately selects a higher-
cost private institution).

Cooperation among institutions, private and public,
must be expedited through a clearing house on facilities, programs, resources, and personnel. Various types of consortia
should be developed. Artificial restrictions on transfer of credits
and residence requirements must be liberalized or eliminated.
All extension and continuing education activities should be
coordinated at state level and perhaps centralized in a single
office.

One or more institutes, centers, or facilities should be
organized at a state level, where the resources of the various
universities can be pooled to make a major attack on some of
the social and economic problems faced by the state.

State boundaries are only historical artifacts as far as
higher education is concerned. Cooperative developments
among states, involving both public and private institutions,
should be encouraged. Not every graduate or professional program is needed in every state. Some type of negotiation is
needed in every state and ultimately at the national level to
delimit the number of graduate schools and graduate professional programs. Some regional facility similar to WICHE
(Western Interstate Commission for Higher Education) or
SREB (Southern Regional Education Board) is needed.

It is appropriate and it is necessary at the state level at
present to decide on institutional roles and to have enough
controls to ensure that these roles are followed. It is appropriate
to demand that institutions engage themselves with the problems of the people from whom they receive support; and when,
as now appears to be the case, the problems transcend the abilities of a single institution, new units may need to be created
and supported to resolve them.

Strong state coordination is essential. But state coordination will be successful only if the coordinating staff is composed
of experienced individuals who engage in planning and de-

veloping principles enforced by occasional review and who refuse to become involved in petty detail and day-to-day operations on the campuses.

9

Where Do We Stand?

Higher education today faces challenge and intervention from several external sources. Universities have been required by the federal government to present programs for correction of discriminatory practices in selection, promotion, and salary rewards for women and minorities as a condition for continuing to receive federal grants. State governments have become concerned with tenure and with faculty load as well as generally with programs and budgets. Judicial rulings have contravened actions with regard to nonreappointment. State-wide coordination imposes role definitions on universities and demands prior approval of major research and service programs supported by external funds as well as of new curricular or degree programs. Multicampus systems move some decisions from local campuses to central administrative offices. External agencies responsible for support of the university are losing faith in the ability of the faculty and the local administration to use funds wisely or to fulfill obligations to society.

Internally, the autonomy of various segments of the

university is also under attack. Minorities and women—as students, faculty, and employees—demand that the university eliminate discriminatory practices and demonstrate equity in its treatment of these groups. Their demands include special courses or curricular provisions: black and Chicano studies, special programs for the disadvantaged, and greater flexibility in admissions. Students and faculty demand more part in decisions directly affecting their welfare as well as in selection of departmental chairmen, institute directors, deans, and other administrators. Institutional governing boards, alerted by these external and internal demands, demonstrate more interest in curriculum, personnel appointments, and allocation of funds. Unions or other organizations of clerical and administrative personnel, as well as of faculty, bargain for new policies in salary adjustments, vacations, promotions, and fringe benefits.

The faculty—faced by external intervention, which threatens faculty prerogatives in determining curriculum, load, evaluation of performance, and reward systems—see the conflict both as a threat to autonomy and an attempt to subjugate their scholarly efforts to utilitarian considerations. Their professional and personal goals seem to conflict with the public interest. The conflict, in an ultimate sense, is for control of the university's value system. Faculty members, on the whole, do not appear willing to share with students and external groups the determination of these values or the modes of attaining them. They do not appear willing to submit to probing performance reviews by persons who may, by faculty standards, lack the competency to define and collect adequate data or to make sound judgments of professional service and performance. The disagreement involves both ends and means. The search for truth in the academy and the educational needs of society represent conflicting conceptions of university goals; and these conflicting conceptions lead to differing conceptions of efficiency, organization, discipline, and authority. Efficiency in the pursuit of truth as seen by the scholar has little to do with costs or economic benefits. The type of organization and governance the scholar sees as consonant with individual autonomy in pursuit of truth is usually more flexible and decentralized than the patterns required for efficiency in fulfilling the educational requirements of society. Discipline to the scholar is provided by the essential characteristics of his topic of study, whereas discipline implies to those concerned with efficiency the adherence to rules and policies which ensure both economical and effective performance.

The present scene in higher education is characterized by these changes: (1) Respect for universities (faculties and administrators) has been replaced by distrust and surveillance. (2) Informal procedures and policies based upon mutual respect and confidence within the university have been replaced by insistence upon due process and by formalized codes. (3) Collegiality based upon unity in goals has been replaced by identification and resolution of conflict. (4) Decentralization of decision making to more homogeneous and unified subgroups is demanded within the university, while simultaneously greater centralization embracing systems of institutions is demanded for budgeting, role determination, and planning. (5) Faculty professionalism is challenged because it represents priorities and concerns for prestige which are inimical to the public interest and because it is irresponsible and unethical in its indifference to undergraduates and its continuing reduction of teaching loads in favor of research.

In reaction to these stresses, governance on the campus is becoming more political in nature. Concerns about who holds the power, how to get a piece of it, or how to influence those who hold it become the center of attention. Faculty and student groups compete with one another to achieve special interests and goals, sometimes joining forces to confront administrators, board members, and external agencies. Discontent is rife; and collective bargaining attracts many faculty members, who see it as the only effective recourse against administrative interference and external intervention.

The resolution of this complex of internal and external issues and pressures is not yet in sight. Certainly new forms of faculty participation in governance must be evolved; these new forms must involve faculty sharing of decision-making prerogatives with others—students, administrators, nonacademic staff,

coordinating boards, and the public. A redefinition of professional and institutional autonomy and of academic freedom
may emerge, a redefinition in which professional values and
misplaced institutional priorities are balanced by awareness and
responsiveness to the values and concerns of the broader society. Neglect of social obligations and inept financial management must certainly be brought under control by performance
review and accountability, which ensure that universities fulfill
their functions efficiently and in accordance with priorities acceptable to those who provide the support. There will never
be unanimity within the university or in the external sources
of support on these issues, any more than there is unity in our
society about other major issues; but higher education can no
longer operate as a small privileged enterprise serving an elite
with little regard for the interests of the general public.

Neither is it any longer possible to accept one model—
the full service graduate and graduate professional university
—as the pattern for which every institution is privileged to
strive. Role determination and evaluation of institutional success in fulfilling assigned roles must replace the caste system
which mistakenly equates university quality with graduate programs, research productivity, and decreased instructional load.

Society supports higher education because of the promise
that higher education holds for improving the quality of our
life. Thus, support of higher education is heavily interwoven
with a concern for the practical significance of education in
enhancing individuals' earning ability as well as their contributions to society. Support of instruction and public-service
activities reasonably and naturally follows from these concerns.
Support of research is less attractive because the results of research—in terms of immediate values to society—are less clear.
But most professors are attracted to higher education as much
if not more by love of the disciplines than by any desire to teach
or to be of service to society. Furthermore, the traditional Ph.D.
program emphasizes research and decries the desirability or
even the possibility of any training or practice which would
directly improve the quality of teaching. To cover up this conflict between social and academic values, the academy has ra-

tionalized that society has an obligation to support the scholar in his search for truth and that the scholar must be granted almost complete freedom to define his own way of life. This same rationale argues that college students from the outset should be so highly motivated that no attention need be given to teaching techniques, learning problems, or evaluation of achievements. In this view, the department and the university exist to nurture the scholar, whose service to his discipline excuses him from loyalty to the institution and from responsibility to society.

Ultimately, the faculty responds to the reward system. Administrators, graduate schools, and the public at large have unwittingly conspired with faculties to accord adulation to universities with strong graduate and professional programs and to reward faculties for research and—as an ironic consequence—for being unresponsive to students or public. No system of incentives exists to make faculties responsive to social needs; changes in structure and reward system will be required to bring this about. At present, faculty members are educated in graduate schools, which ignore teaching and enshrine research, and the reward system of colleges and universities operates in a similar manner. Departments control resources and develop programs; but specialized departmental faculty members have no interest in the total curriculum of the undergraduate; they usually have no competence for planning such a curriculum; they often have reasonable doubts that they will be rewarded (except by administrative appointment) for such activity; and they can see that curriculum expertise is not highly regarded in the academic market. This combination of factors (especially the last two) makes it almost impossible to create a nondepartmental undergraduate program.

Certainly there should be a number (surely no more than 100 to 150) of first-class graduate and research universities in which outstanding scholars are given full support. But most university and college faculty members are not doing research and are not really interested in it. Even in the elite universities some faculty members who pretend to do research only putter around the fringes of insignificant problems. The task of defining "productive" research is difficult, but the myth that all "research" activity is worthwhile must be rejected. In most university departments, only a few research scholars make contributions that justify a restricted teaching load of one or two courses. This is no excuse for reducing everyone's load in vain expectation that all will do research. Faculty researchers contend that undergraduates should be taught by those who are doing research and reinforce their contention with claims that the major is the most important factor in the undergraduate program and that researchers are the best teachers. There is no sound evidence to support these claims. As colleges and universities turn their attention to undergraduate programs based upon problems or themes transcending the disciplines, it becomes obvious that the specialized Ph.D., with its emphasis on research, is one of the main hazards to the development of innovative undergraduate programs.

The size and expense of the higher education enterprise indicate that only a limited number of institutions already fully developed as graduate and professional universities can be granted autonomy in programs and in modes of execution of them. This autonomy remains contingent on demonstration of effective and efficient performance. The autonomy of other institutions must be curtailed by role assignments and continuing review, which prevent them from slighting their assigned role in an attempt to achieve the enshrined research- and graduate-oriented model. Our survey of opinions about autonomy (reported in Chapter Three) suggests that significant percentages of faculty probably would accept this view of constrained autonomy.

In the face of these external forces, the importance of reconsideration of internal campus governance cannot be overestimated. Campus governance which assumes that the institution is being run for the benefit of the faculty rather than of society is doomed to fail. Some balance will have to be found between centralization and decentralization. This is true within the university; it is true in state systems of universities; and it is true with the whole system of higher education in the United States.

NEEDED: A NEW SOCIAL ROLE

Observers of higher education have often pointed out serious flaws in our operations, while reformers have made many unheeded pleas for new approaches. Earl McGrath (1959) once titled a monograph "The Graduate School and the Decline of Liberal Education," which suggests that one of higher education's current problems has been around for some time. In all of the innovative organizations in England and the United States, there is a very grave threat that, in the long run, the graduate school specialization of new faculty will erode the original characteristics of the innovation. Within the last few years discussions of the Doctor of Arts degree offer some promise that a new pattern of training for undergraduate education—a pattern that is broader in its conception and more related to the needs of society and of undergraduate students—may be developed. Yet there is evidence in many institutions that have adopted the Doctor of Arts degree that the departments have specified requirements almost identical to those of the Ph.D. Few students are likely to risk a degree of possibly lower prestige which is so little different from the Ph.D. This conservative model of the D.A. insisted upon by faculties is not likely to solve the problem of improving undergraduate education. Interest in the D.A. degree suggests the need for reorganizing graduate schools to provide for problem-oriented and inter-disciplinary-based doctorates, but departments and their faculties display little interest in such change.

Indeed, most faculty members and departments seem to have operated on the principle that what is good for them is good for the university; and, in turn, the university seems to have operated on the principle that what is good for the university is good for society. But, in fact, what they perceive as good for the university is not necessarily needed by, wanted by, or good for society.

Faculties have been described as individual entrepreneurs who enjoy complete market control. While it pains one to extend the economic market analogy too far into the world of the intellectual, there is no reason to believe that academicians or intellectuals are any more or less selfish, conservative, or cantankerous than other human beings. It is difficult in these circumstances to imagine that faculties unperturbed by any force other than their own perceptions are likely to push for radical change in the status quo.

Administrators, particularly those who view themselves or actually behave as agents of the faculty, find themselves in a weak position to exert leadership in situations requiring radical power, especially in a period of expanding faculty power. Students by and large are not and probably will not be strategically located in the decision-making structure of the universities. Moreover, students as a group do not share so common a point of view on reform issues as is usually assumed and their transitory status tends to militate against the development of a sustained and consistent effort.

Institutional structures and mechanisms, informal as well as formal, must be adapted to the social functions to be performed. The undergraduate college and the research-oriented graduate training institute both perform distinct and honorable functions.

Both deserve the best support we can give them, but it is clear that there are more functions to be performed in higher education than these and other institutions presently acknowledge, and that norms in certain key areas—compensation, job security, credentials, and curricula—should not be the same in each. We jeopardize the health of all educational institutions if we do not make the effort to match their functions, with adjusted modes of operation, to the most urgent social and educational needs [Dungan, 1970, p. 152].

Fundamentally, universities need to clarify their own purposes in performing appropriate and necessary functions for society. This task is difficult because there are several competing views about the university's role in society. Those who see its task as the search for truth usually accept as an addendum that it is also responsible for evaluating the culture itself. The search for truth provides the basis for questioning everything, and theoretically the university can do this without becoming involved in problems of society or functioning as a change agent. In this pattern, academic freedom is not a serious problem because most of society does not understand what is going on in the university and is not perturbed by what emanates from it.

A second possible role involves the university directly in service to society, training persons for professional roles and seeking solutions for the problems of society. It may even go beyond that role to an active involvement of faculty, students, and administrators in the problems of society. This role projects the university onto the political scene, probably with repercussions that affect the support of the institution. Taxes imposed on philanthropic foundations just a year or two ago indicated the reaction of legislators to expenditures and involvements on the political scene, of which they do not approve. The line between social and political action is not always clear. The university trains physicians without taking a position on socialized medicine. But the reactions of radical students in the recent past to ROTC on campus suggests that the separation between educational programs and social policy is not clear to everyone concerned.

It will not be easy to introduce into the university programs focused on social problems, even though there is a clear need for new types of trained professionals to deal with some of these problems. J. Kenneth Hare (Steinhart and Cherniack, 1969, 5, 6) professor of geography at the University of British Columbia, comments:

> Let me start, then, with the question of environmental studies in the modern university. . . . The status quo is defended in depth by the vested interests of a large number of able people. Among these interests are those of the traditional departments and the largely analytical disciplines they profess. Also strong are the numerous special institutes and centers. . . . When we propose to start up a broad-spectrum, synthesizing effort like environmental studies we run full tilt into all these vested interests. We also bank ourselves against the clan spirit of the traditional faculty groupings. . . . Environmental studies have to involve many of these clans, which are not used to combining in the way required. If we suggest, as I do, that some of them—notably the humanists—may be utterly transformed by such combinations we alarm the timid and anger the Tories among them. . . .

The political interest in the environment demands proposals for *action*. . . . At present we are not equipped to make such proposals. We are not action-oriented and on every campus is a deadweight of opinion that regards action-oriented programs as hostile to the academic life. . . .

Hare might have gone on to point out that, were a university to identify large corporations' or local municipalities' contributions to pollution, some difficulties would surely arise. Some universities have avoided this by becoming preoccupied with problems at the national or international level, thereby decreasing the need to accommodate themselves to local pressures. But this leads to poor relations with the local community, which then begins to wonder why it should provide support for an institution that makes so little contribution to the local program.

The task of redefining the social role and purposes of higher education will not be easily accomplished and may never be fully accomplished. But the modern university has become so involved in its own self-fulfillment that it has ignored its social obligations and distorted its purposes and priorities. To regain that confidence requires at least three steps (Cheit, 1971). First, the universities must demonstrate that they can maintain peace and quiet on campus and concentrate on scholarly matters. Second, they must demonstrate that they can maintain some efficiency in their operations and gain the cooperation of faculty and students in so doing. Third, they must redefine purposes, priorities, and relationships with society in ways that the society itself can understand and accept.

The large numbers of universities, the extensive range of their educational programs, and the growing drain they make on the public purse require that individual universities recognize themselves as part of a larger system of institutions of higher education—state, regional, and national. Their ambitions and aspirations must be modified to improve their total effort. Yet too many efforts at institutional cooperation are trivial; significant cooperation has been achieved only when collaboration has produced new resources. Effective cooperation on a broader scale will require strong coordination. Universities will gain in public confidence if they recognize the necessity for coordination and accept it. The autonomy of universities will be constrained, preferably by an increased sense of social responsibility but certainly by public demand and intervention by those who provide the resources.

Both university autonomy and academic freedom, like other freedoms, have limits imposed both by professional responsibility and by the society to which the university must be responsive. In fact, constrained autonomy is the natural state of the university. Faculty, students, and administrators are all constrained by policy statements and procedural requirements, as well as by humane, professional, and political considerations. The idea that students or faculty, separately or in combination, should make all decisions that affect their own lives is appealing but unreasonable insofar as their decisions affect others. Limits have been and will continue to be placed upon the decisions that faculty members can make about students; but students cannot be relied upon to make all decisions about their own education. Conflicts of interest among and between faculty and students require constraints on both.

Constraints requiring judgments about individual behavior portend an expenditure of time, energy, and emotion, as well as subsequent controversy, which may prejudice the application of constraints. Hence, the characteristics of constraints—their necessity, justifiability, enforceability, and equitability—have great import. The attempted remedy can be worse than the affliction.

ASPECTS OF CONSTRAINTS

We are concerned with two basic questions about constraints. When are constraints justifiable? What types of constraints are justifiable? Generally, constraints are justifiable when they (a) tend to make students' educational experience more interesting, challenging, and relevant to social needs; (b) provide policies that are both necessary and fair as judged by students and the general public; (c) encourage or ensure more efficient use of resources; (d) permit effectiveness and success to be judged by results and by costs, rather than by faculty or student preference for particular educational processes. These justifications place constraints in their most desirable light. For constraints to be regarded as fair, they must be justified by circumstances and results, they must be interpretable under varying conditions, and any penalties or sanctions for violation must be appropriate. The issue is Who decides what is reasonable? Clearly, faculty or students acting separately or together cannot, because of conflicts of interest, always be permitted to make this decision.

Penalties for violation place constraints in the most undesirable light, especially when applied to individuals. When the corporate university refuses to assent to role assignments and new program denials, it can be brought to terms by budget reductions. However, when an individual refuses to accept what his colleagues agree is a reasonable teaching assignment, he will not easily be terminated; nor is it likely that alternative sanctions, such as withholding salary increments, will be supported. Reducing the departmental budget could become the ultimate penalty to force departmental action.

Constraints may be unqualified and rigidly applied; for example, a demand that every faculty member have not less than a certain number of classroom contact hours. If classroom contact hours are precisely defined, then the only flexibility left is in the extent to which faculty members are willing or required to take on teaching and other responsibilities beyond that minimum; over time, the minimum will become the maximum. An average contact hour load requirement permits individual adjustments for other responsibilities or the demands of particular types of teaching. But as the restriction becomes less specific (every individual is expected to carry a reasonable or minimal teaching load), its interpretation and administration become more and more highly judgmental; and the problem of enforcement becomes more difficult.

When educational experiences are evaluated without evidence of quality differences between units or institutions, those who are concerned with efficiency and costs are tempted to impose uniform quantitative standards. Constraints requiring demonstration of the attainment of higher standards are found in contracts that pay off in accordance with gains made by students or the percentage of students attaining the standard in a given period of time. However, to ask any professional to guarantee results places him in an unethical position and imposes risks that would promote a different kind of irresponsibility—the attempt to achieve results by teaching for the test or by some even more dishonest procedure.

There is a significant distinction between externally and internally imposed constraints. The individual who imposes his own set of constraints exercises his freedom and demonstrates responsibility. When individuals and institutions fail to exhibit social responsibility, external agencies impose constraints. Constraints should definitely not be externally imposed on such matters as course titles, textbooks, specifications of equipment, course credits, patterns of instruction and organization, and transferability of courses and credits. Nevertheless, calendars have been prescribed and some staffing formulas come close to defining organizational and instructional patterns. External constraint carried to extremes is counterproductive. It may save a few dollars here and there, but it forces faculty into a routine more appropriate (although still questionable) for elementary or secondary school teachers than for college and university professors. Such detailed prescription also denies students the educational alternatives available when faculty members have freedom to develop their own courses and their own approaches to them. Individualization of education is threatened by excesses in external constraint just as surely as it has been by the excessive autonomy which led to the constraints.

The essential form of constraint in state systems of higher education is the definition of roles for each private and public institution. To determine the role of an institution, it is necessary to have a plan for the state or region, taking into account total resources and educational needs. Each institution must have an assigned range of programs and a degree level (baccalaureate, master's, or doctoral) that it is permitted to offer. The acceptance of state or federal dollars by private institutions surely obligates them also to accept the combination of private and public institutions as a single system.

Such role definition will call for some cooperation between state and federal government. Federal funding of institutional aspirations has not, at times, been consistent with a state plan. State-supported institutions will argue that, if external funding is found, no state plan should delimit or deny their use of funds. Unfortunately, external funding is often temporary, and new program costs ultimately fall back upon the institution.

Universities that are primarily graduate professional and research institutions would benefit by role definitions, since they would be protected against the dilution of resources which results when all institutions attempt to attain that same character. And the other institutions would be protected against themselves. Their aspirations to a wide variety of new programs and new levels of education without adequate justification in need or available finances could be effectively curbed. Only externally imposed role definitions will resolve the problem.

Institutional role designation merges into constraints on curriculum, since the designation of programs offered by level (undergraduate or graduate) and by field (liberal arts, engineering, education) defines the institutional role. Maintenance of institutional roles requires continuing review of all new program proposals in reference to need, availability of funds, and appropriateness of location. The information demanded for an adequate review is, in itself, a boon to institutions in which curriculum expansion has proceeded with little planning. Producing the required information and demonstrating need will eliminate a few program proposals, but the coordinating board will still need to review and validate the information submitted: staff competency, library holdings, facilities, equipment, and—especially—added costs. Institutional aspirations readily lead to biased appraisals of present resources, societal needs, and future costs.

A coordinating council should avoid review of specific courses. The task is much too detailed and time-consuming. Nevertheless, occasional review of course offerings and proposed additions may provide omens of intentions. Advanced science or engineering courses, which require specific laboratory space, equipment, and a highly specialized professor, are expensive for small enrollments. On most campuses there is undue repetition of courses from one term to another. Even on large university campuses the percentages of small classes (fewer than fifteen students) may startle both faculty and administrators, who are used to students' complaints about large classes. Such data can show that some institutions, despite their protests to the contrary, do not really need new resources but need to reassign existing ones.

Coordination should be limited to developing guiding rules or principles, coupled with an injunction for annual reports on certain categories of course offerings and credit patterns. Awareness that these practices may have budgetary implications can provide the local campus with just the weapon that its administrators need to force faculty to review them.

Tenure can reinforce faculty irresponsibility because it permits the faculty to ignore criticism while pursuing whatever gives them the most satisfaction. Whatever the eulogies written about it, tenure implies an emphasis on job security. In a sense, acquiescence to the combined demands for academic freedom and tenure makes the academic gown a magic cloak which can transform some mice into lions. Professors can make statements irrelevant to their expertise with no worry about reprimand or reprisal. Faculties have exhibited little responsibility in disciplining erring colleagues. Some individuals faced with non-reappointment or nonpromotion have deliberately engaged in irresponsible behavior in full expectation that an appeal to the concept of academic freedom will arouse colleagues and secure tenure or promotion. Academia has too often become a haven for the opinionated, the eccentric, and the disruptive.

Sufficient professional autonomy must be retained to allow professors to define goals, activities, and standards of evaluation for their students and to prevent complete standardization and routinization. The scholarly way of life requires freedom in scheduling work time, since creativity cannot be turned on or off like water from a tap. Externally imposed red tape must be minimized. Routine and detailed reporting of one's activities is antithetical to scholarship. A sufficient measure of autonomy and of academic freedom must be maintained to prevent turning the professor into a time clock employee.

Institutions fear that coordination may only add another echelon of authority with increased red tape and costs but with no advantages to the institutions. If coordinating boards are willing to determine institutional roles and hold institutions to them, the fully developed universities and the public will clearly gain. The fully developed universities will no longer need to fear loss of resources to aspiring regional institutions. The public will be relieved of the burden of rising costs caused by proliferation of unneeded programs.

If coordinating boards are to accomplish their goals, their prestige must be such that political intervention in board recommendations becomes almost impossible. Coordinating boards will have to move their focus from input to output accountability. At present we have little evidence on output per se and almost none on the influence of input on output. A normal tendency is to stress uniformity in input patterns and to minimize costs. Quantification is another frequently cited path to accountability. But while degrees produced are quantifiable output in a limited sense, sheer numbers can give no account of quality. In fact, manipulation of input and requirements can markedly increase numbers of degrees and may increase or decrease quality. Definitions of courses, credit hours, or faculty size are quantifiable, but usually in ways idiosyncratic to institutions. However, until both input and output are described and measured objectively, no valid mechanisms can be developed for relating input and output. Qualitative evaluation by public agencies might provide more satisfactory evidence than other methods but the difficulties of such evaluation, as well as faculty and institutional aversion to it, make its ultimate benefits doubtful.

Universities' major gains from coordination may be restricted to less political intervention, less competition on campus for program expansion and innovation, clearer institutional purposes, and possibly better support because of the unified and more credible presentation of budget requests.

To administrators and faculty accustomed to the autonomy of the individual campus and to the competitive approach which has so long characterized the university, the recommendations in this volume may constitute a major threat. Although that threat may be interpreted as a threat to autonomy and therefore to quality, the real threat is to the aspirations of the individuals and the institution. The luxury of autonomy for individual institutions can no longer be tolerated. It was appropriate, perhaps, for an earlier day, when the development of higher education was still in its adolescence, concerned with the establishment of various types of institutions where numbers were not large, and usually limited to the elite. In the present day, higher education must be regarded as a state and a national resource and must be coordinated and controlled so as to fulfill the needs of society.

Appendix A:
Facsimile of the Survey

Separate versions of the questionnaire were prepared for the four main groups in the survey population: legislators, board members, administrators, and faculty members. The differences were mainly in the identification items at the top of page 2. On pages 2 and 3, the faculty members' version had additional items 3.i. and 6. Pages 4 through 7 were identical for all four groups. The version presented here is the one sent to faculty members.

Departmental Study Project * Office of Institutional Research * Michigan State University * East Lansing, Michigan 48823

DIRECTOR

Paul L. Dressel
Assistant Provost
Director of Institutional Research

ASSISTANT DIRECTOR

William H. Faricy

CONSULTANTS

Philip M. Marcus
Associate Professor
Department of Sociology

F. Craig Johnson
Professor and Research Associate
The Florida State University

March 10, 1971

Dear Colleague:

Today's turmoil in the universities results at least partly from our lack of knowledge of the institutions of higher education. With this questionnaire we are trying to increase our knowledge by surveying the operations of university departments across the country. This effort is part of a research project supported by an ESSO Education Foundation grant.

The enclosed questionnaire is one of the instruments being used in this study. We would like you to fill out the form completely and then to make comments on the last page for any points which you wish to question, emphasize, or add. We estimate that this form should take only about 30 minutes.

We would greatly appreciate receiving your reply within a week. For your convenience a self-addressed envelope is enclosed.

196

Your responses will be treated in complete confidence. No person, department, or university will ever be identified in any way in any report.

If you would like a summary statement of the final report of our study, please send us your name and address on a separate postcard and we shall mail you a copy as soon as it is available.

We are sure that you will be willing to devote a few minutes to helping this study. Your opinions and suggestions will be very valuable to us. The back page has been left blank for you to use for your comments.

We thank you for your cooperation.

Sincerely yours,

Paul L. Dressel

Questionnaire

What is your present rank? (Check one)

_____ Professor _____ Associate professor _____ Assistant professor _____ Other (please specify) _____

What is your main departmental affiliation? _____
(Write in one department name)
Name of your university. (Write in) _____

If you are a department chairman or head, please check here _____

1. Within your department how much emphasis is actually placed upon each of the following? (Check one on each line)

	Very great amount	Great amount	Some	Slight amount	None at all
a. Undergraduate instruction	_____	_____	_____	_____	_____
b. Graduate instruction	_____	_____	_____	_____	_____
c. Basic research	_____	_____	_____	_____	_____
d. Contributing to the discipline studied in your department	_____	_____	_____	_____	_____
e. Service to business, industry, or government	_____	_____	_____	_____	_____

2. From the list in item 1 above, select the one item you feel should receive the most emphasis in universities generally.

(Write the letter in the space below)

_____ should receive the most emphasis.

3. In general, how much influence does each of the following have over what goes on in your department? (Check one on each line)

	Very great influence	Great influence	Some influence	Slight influence	No influence at all
a. The department faculty as a whole	_____	_____	_____	_____	_____
b. The dean of this college or school	_____	_____	_____	_____	_____
c. The department head or chairman	_____	_____	_____	_____	_____
d. Graduate students	_____	_____	_____	_____	_____
e. Undergraduates	_____	_____	_____	_____	_____
f. The university administration (president, vice-presidents)	_____	_____	_____	_____	_____
g. You, personally	_____	_____	_____	_____	_____
h. All-university groups (committees, senate)	_____	_____	_____	_____	_____
i. Department committees	_____	_____	_____	_____	_____

199

4. Within your university, how much difference of opinion exists between the central administration and the departments (or similar units) with regard to the matters listed below? (Check one blank on each line)

	Very great difference of opinion	Great difference of opinion	Some difference of opinion	Slight difference of opinion	No difference of opinion
a. Hiring practices	___	___	___	___	___
b. Promotion practices	___	___	___	___	___
c. Salary decisions	___	___	___	___	___
d. Curriculum innovation	___	___	___	___	___
e. Teaching loads	___	___	___	___	___
f. Financial allocations	___	___	___	___	___
g. Course offerings	___	___	___	___	___

5. Some people have said that what is good for the department is good for the university as a whole. To what extent do you agree with this statement? (Check one)

_____ To a very great extent

_____ To a great extent

_____ To some extent

_____ To a slight extent

_____ To no extent at all

6. In general, do you usually think of yourself primarily as a member of your: (Check one)

_____ University

_____ Department

_____ Discipline

201

On page 5, opposite, actions or decisions usually initiated in university departments are listed. For each action, please indicate your opinion as to the **highest** level at which an action could be justifiably reviewed with authority to veto it.

While making your choices, consider them in terms of an **ideal** situation, **not** your actual situation.

In Column A on page 5: Please write the number of the organizational level from List I, below, to indicate the **highest** level at which departmental actions could justifiably be reviewed with authority for final veto.

In Column B on page 5: Please write the number of a statement from List II, below, to indicate the **one** best justification for the veto authority you have indicated in Column A.

LIST I

Levels of Organization
Use these items in Column A on page 5

1. Individual faculty member
2. Department (chairman or faculty committees)
3. College or School (dean or faculty committees)
4. All-university faculty committees
5. Administration (president, vice-presidents)
6. Trustees, governing board
*7. Central administration of a multicampus institution
*8. Public officials or Legislatures
9. No review at all.

These levels of organizations will not apply to most private institutions.

(Please write only one number for each item in Column A.)

LIST II

Justification for review/veto authority
Use these items in Column B on page 5

1. Welfare of total faculty
2. Welfare of students
3. Academic freedom
4. Improvement in quality of education
5. Advancement of a discipline or profession
6. Efficient use of financial or human resources
7. Assigned role in a multicampus system
8. Counterbalance to departments' self-interest
9. Uniform practice and policy in a university
10. Other reasons

(Please write only one number for each item in Column B.)

202

Departmental Actions	Column A Highest Level of Review	Column B Justification
1. Adding a new course for majors		
2. Adding a new undergraduate degree program		
3. Type of instruction used (lecture, discussion, etc.)		
4. Class or section size		
5. Adding a new course (service) for nonmajors		
6. Time of class meetings		
7. Course requirements (papers) exams, attendance, etc.)		
8. Adding a new graduate degree program		
9. Reading assignments for a course		
10. Adequacy and fairness of grading system		
11. Use of computer services		
12. Class credit or contact hours assigned to a professor		
13. Reduction in teaching assignments for research or service		
14. Tenure appointment of a faculty member		
15. Amount of time permitted for paid off-campus consultation		
16. Nonreappointment of a non-tenured faculty member		

Departmental Actions	Column A Highest Level of Review	Column B Justification
17. Policies affecting nonacademic personnel		
18. Defining tenure criteria		
19. Determining salary for a faculty member		
20. Criteria for admitting undergraduate major students		
21. Authorizing professors' travel paid from departmental funds		
22. Applications for research grants made by departmental faculty members		
23. Number of undergraduate major students admitted		
24. Selecting departmental chairman		

Departmental Actions	Column A Highest Level of Review	Column B Justification
25. Determining faculty participation in departmental governance		
26. Adding a variant of an existing course		
27. Number of graduate students admitted to department		
28. Number and length of class meetings		
29. Allocating expenses of various accounts		
30. Assigning teachers to courses		
31. Determining student participation in departmental governance		
32. Approving expenditures for guest speakers		

The following statements express opinions about universities that one encounters today. To what extent do you agree with these statements? (Check one blank on each line)

	Very great agreement	Great agreement	Some agreement	Slight agreement	No agreement
1. Infringements on departmental autonomy imply a denial of professional competency.	_____	_____	_____	_____	_____
2. Departments exist to carry out university policy.	_____	_____	_____	_____	_____
3. University autonomy is essential to preserve intellectual creativity.	_____	_____	_____	_____	_____
4. Incursions into a university's autonomy are justified when a university operates inefficiently.	_____	_____	_____	_____	_____
5. Governing boards must establish minimum teaching loads to insure that professors are in the classroom.	_____	_____	_____	_____	_____
6. A major reason for infringing on university autonomy lies in the lack of understanding of educational matters by laymen.	_____	_____	_____	_____	_____

	Very great agreement	Great agreement	Some agreement	Slight agreement	No agreement
7. Basic conflicts of interest between departments and their university require monitoring by others outside the university.	___	___	___	___	___
8. The department chairman's role should include protecting his faculty against infringements on department autonomy.	___	___	___	___	___
9. If faculty were more attentive to instructional problems, student pressure on administrations would lessen.	___	___	___	___	___
10. Incursions into a department's autonomy are justified when a department operates inefficiently.	___	___	___	___	___
11. Legislatures have the right to set minimum instructional loads for the faculty of public-supported universities.	___	___	___	___	___
12. Departmental autonomy is essential to insure the highest quality of education.	___	___	___	___	___

206

	Very great agreement	Great agreement	Some agreement	Slight agreement	No agreement
13. Universities generally are trying to do more than their available resources can support.	____	____	____	____	____
14. A very high degree of specialization by professors requires universities to limit departmental autonomy.	____	____	____	____	____
15. University administrators do not exert enough control over faculty work load.	____	____	____	____	____
16. The faculty usually tries to increase research time at the expense of time that should be spent on teaching.	____	____	____	____	____
17. Operation of the university should be turned over to the faculty.	____	____	____	____	____

Various ways are being suggested today to increase the universities' prestige and credibility with the general public. Please indicate your reaction to each of these possible ways.

| 18. — Maintain firm student discipline on campus. | ____ | ____ | ____ | ____ | ____ |

	Very great agreement	Great agreement	Some agreement	Slight agreement	No agreement
19. — Reduce the university's budget.	___	___	___	___	___
20. — Provide more and better services to the community.	___	___	___	___	___
21. — Demonstrate that the university's educational output actually justifies the input of resources.	___	___	___	___	___
22. — Increase the university's communications with all of its clienteles (students, parents, alumni, taxpayers, businessmen, et al.).	___	___	___	___	___
23. — Rationalize and streamline the university's organizational structure.	___	___	___	___	___
24. — Create new programs and courses suitable to our present society.	___	___	___	___	___
25. — Involve students more closely in governance of the university.	___	___	___	___	___

26. — Make the governing board's membership more representative of the total community served by the university.

Very great agreement	Great agreement	Some agreement	Slight agreement	No agreement

Appendix B:
Survey Population

SELECTION OF UNIVERSITIES

For this survey we considered only universities that are comprehensive,[1] since problems of departmental autonomy are more marked in universities than in liberal-arts colleges. In comprehensive universities, the differing needs of undergraduate instruction, graduate instruction, and research; the availability of outside funding; and social pressures from many sources produce tensions within the institution as well as demands from outside for constraints.

Ideally this study would have been based on a stratified random sample, but that procedure seemed inappropriate, since American universities are not distributed uniformly in terms of any relevant variables. We sought to define a population reasonably representative of American universities based on the following characteristics: geographical region, type of control,

[1] The group we refer to is type "IV-K" in the classification developed by the U.S. Office of Education and used in the *American Universities and Colleges,* tenth edition, pp. 1720 ff.: institutions offering the Ph.D. and equivalent degree, with liberal arts and general programs, and three or more professional schools. The total group includes 128 universities.

size of student body, caliber of educational resources, and prestige of graduate school. (Caliber and prestige appeared to affect respondents' opinions in approximately the same manner. Therefore, in the text we have reported the analysis only in terms of prestige, for the sake of simplicity.)

We defined four *regions:* East, South, Midwest, and West. This division seemed close to common usage and presented no problems in assigning institutions to regions. By *control* we mean an institution's legal status as a private or public corporation. *Size* we defined as the full-time-student enrollment, with three levels: small—less than 8,000; medium— 8,000 to 16,000; and large—more than 16,000. (Enrollment figures are from Parker, 1972).

For *caliber* of educational resources we used two measures: (1) a university's general-fund expenditures per full-time student (Singletary, 1968), and (2) the ratio of full-time faculty to full-time students (Parker, 1972). With these two measures we ranked the universities previously identified and divided the group at the median. To measure graduate school *prestige* we used the "Cartter Report" (Cartter, 1966) to construct a ranking based on a combination of the universities' ratings for graduate faculty and programs, divided at the median into high and low groups. We had completed this process before the 1970 ACE report of graduate education (Roose and Andersen, 1970) was available; but after checking our selection against the more recent ratings, we found the only change indicated thereby was addition of another university.

The number of universities in each of the categories defined for this population is shown in Table 7.

POPULATION OF INTEREST

The recipients of our questionnaire can be viewed as a nonrandom sample drawn from a nonnormally distributed population, or as a population in itself. Since the hazards of generalization would be about equal in either case—namely, high—we shall take the simpler alternative and refer to our group as a population. Our readers generalize to other populations at their own risk.

TABLE 7. UNIVERSITIES SELECTED FOR THE SURVEY (TOTAL = 42)

Characteristics		Number of Universities in Category	Per Cent of Total Universities	Response Rate [a]	Per Cent of Total Respondents
Region	East	11	26%	38%	24%
	Midwest	10	24	43	29
	South	11	26	44	20
	West	10	24	40	27
Control	Private	25	40	40.5	30
	Public	17	60	41.5	69
Size	Small	12	28	45	18
	Medium	10	24	41	23
	Large	20	48	39	59
Educational Caliber	Higher	21	50	38.6	52
	Lower	21	50	43	48
Graduate Prestige	Higher	21	50	36.5	58
	Lower	21	50	45	42

[a] Response rate is the per cent of the questionnaires mailed that were returned by individuals at institutions in the various categories listed at left.

To select the legislators to be surveyed, we asked the legislative clerk in each state for the membership list of the education committees of both houses. Our mailing list consisted of all the names on the lists we received from thirty-six states. That number seemed large enough, so we made no further efforts to contact the states not replying.

We took the names of university board members, administrators, and faculty members from the most recent directories or catalogs available to us. The mailing list included the entire staff listed for each of the nine departments previously selected to be surveyed, at each university. Only a few universities did not have all nine departments. The names of the chief administrators from president to dean (excluding librarians and others whose interests are mostly tangential to the departments) and those persons listed as members of the governing board were also included. Seven of the nine disciplines represented by this population are the same as those studied in the previous survey (see *The Confidence Crisis*): chemistry, electrical engineering, English, history, management, mathematics, and psychology. To broaden the representation for this survey, we added economics and botany (or biology, according to a university's usage). The faculty population represented 354 particular departments.

The number of questionnaires mailed out and the response rates are presented in Table 8.

TABLE 8. SURVEY POPULATION AND RESPONSE RATE

	Number of Question- naires Mailed	Number of Question- naires Returned	Response Rate	Per Cent of Total Responding Population
Faculty members	9,952	3,905	40%	87%
Administrators	762	343	45	8
Board members	649	83	13	2
Legislators	968	153	16	3
Total	12,331	4,484	36	
Departments				
Biology/Botany	897	392	43%	10% a
Chemistry	1,101	497	45	13
Economics	932	338	36	9
Electrical Engr.	932	350	37	9
English	1,670	617	37	16
History	1,187	438	37	11
Management	451	191	42	5
Mathematics	1,476	492	33	13
Psychology	1,306	508	39	13

a Per cent of total faculty.

RESPONSE RATE AND CHARACTER

Our first step in distributing the questionnaire was to send each person on the mailing list a letter describing our project and stating that a questionnaire would follow shortly. The second step was mailing the questionnaire. For the third step, about two weeks after mailing the questionnaire we sent a follow-up postcard to the entire mailing list (asking those who had already responded to ignore the card). Thus, we mailed three items to each individual on the list. Since we did not ask respondents to identify themselves by name, we had no further means of directly contacting nonrespondents.

Our overall response rate for university personnel compares favorably with the rate Gross and Grambsch (1968) achieved. Addressing a similar group and using similar techniques to spur responses (although with the advantage of being able to identify nonrespondents for a second mailing of the questionnaire), they had responses from 50.9 per cent of the administrators and 40.4 per cent of the faculty. Their higher response from administrators may result from their somewhat greater efforts to reach that group compared with ours; on the other hand, it may be that administrators were less harried five or six years ago.

When we applied a Kruskal-Wallis test to the response rates, to determine whether the various categories of respondents or universities represented different populations, we found the differences significant only for comparisons of university *caliber* and *prestige*. The response rates at universities that are higher or lower relative to these characteristics were sufficiently different to suggest that caliber and prestige differentiate institutional types. However, as we have pointed out in the text, these variables made little difference in the content of responses to this questionnaire.

These findings suggest that universities with relatively lower resources and prestige are more likely to respond to a survey like the present one than the "big-time" universities. Also, although the differences were not significant, our analysis indicates that persons at smaller universities tend to respond at a greater rate than those at larger ones.

Another provocative finding is that the religious-affiliated universities (three Protestant, four Roman Catholic) were all above the median in response rate. Perhaps personnel at such institutions take their social responsibilities more seriously than most academics; or perhaps those institutions actually form a separate universe, as Gross and Grambsch (1968, p. 19) suggest.

A vexing and perhaps ultimately serious aspect of this survey was the distribution of the questionnaires by mail. This process is not only expensive but apparently untrustworthy as well. Since respondents did not identify themselves on the questionnaire, we could not check them off our mailing list and thus had no way of finding out whether nonrespondents had ever received a questionnaire. When envelopes came back to us marked "address unknown," we occasionally wondered whether they had been returned by personnel who did not bother to look up correct addresses. The unpleasant possibility that many questionnaires were not reaching addresses occurred to us later, after we had mailed the reminder postcards. We received a number of letters saying that the writer had received the postcard (and sometimes the presurvey letter) but never the questionnaire itself. We are grateful to those respondents who were so generous as to write us for a questionnaire. But we were also dismayed to think that many of our efforts might have been to no avail.

Bibliography

"AAUP Gears Up to New Challenges." *Academe,* June 1971, p. 1.

ABRAM, M. B. "Reflections on the University in the New Revolution." In S. R. Graubard and G. A. Ballotti (Eds.), *The Embattled University.* New York: George Braziller, 1970.

ADAMS, R. F., and MICHAELSEN, J. B. *Assessing the Benefits of Collegiate Structure: The Case at Santa Cruz.* Berkeley: Office of the Vice President—Planning and Analysis, University of California, February 1971.

ALTBACH, P. G. "Commitment and Powerlessness on the American Campus: The Case of the Graduate Student." *Liberal Education,* 1960, *56* (4), 562–582.

American Academy of Arts and Sciences. *The Assembly on University Goals and Governance.* Boston, 1971.

ASHBY, E. "Split Personality in Universities." In *Technology and the Academics.* London: Macmillan & Co. Ltd., 1959, 67–97.

BAADE, H. W. (Ed.) *Academic Freedom: The Scholar's Place in Modern Society.* Dobbs Ferry, N. Y.: Oceana Publications, Inc., 1964.

BAILEY, S. K. "Public Money and the Integrity of the Higher Academy." *Educational Record,* 1969, *50*(2), 149–154.

BALDRIDGE, J. V. (Ed.) *Academic Governance.* Berkeley: McCutchan, 1971.

"Bargaining Agents." *The Chronicle of Higher Education,* 1971, *5*(31), 1.

216

BASKIN, S. (Ed.) *Higher Education: Some Newer Developments.* New York: McGraw-Hill, 1965.

BELL, D. "By Whose Right?" In H. L. Hodgkinson and L. R. Meeth (Eds.), *Power and Authority.* San Francisco: Jossey-Bass, 1971.

BELL, D. "Governance of Universities in the 1970s." In S. R. Graubard and G. A. Ballotti (Eds.), *The Embattled University.* New York: George Braziller, 1970.

BELL, D. *The Reforming of General Education.* New York: Columbia University Press, 1966.

BENNIS, W. G. "The Coming Death of Bureaucracy." In L. H. Browder, Jr. (Ed.), *Emerging Patterns of Administrative Accountability.* Berkeley: McCutchan, 1971.

BERDAHL, R. O. *Statewide Coordination of Higher Education.* Washington, D.C.: American Council on Education, 1971.

BOLMAN, F. DEW. "Problems of Change and Changing Problems." *The Journal of Higher Education,* 1970, *41*(8), 589–598.

BROWDER, L. H., JR. "A Thought Collage." In *Emerging Patterns of Administrative Accountability.* Berkeley: McCutchan, 1971.

BROWDER, L. H., JR. (Ed.) *Emerging Patterns of Administrative Accountability.* Berkeley: McCutchan, 1971.

BROWN, R. S., and KUGLER, I. "Collective Bargaining for the Faculty." *Liberal Education,* 1970, *56*(1), 75–85.

BUCHANAN, J. M. "Taxpayer Constraints on Financing Education." In R. L. Johns, I. J. Goffman, K. Alexander, D. H. Stollar (Eds.), *Economic Factors Affecting the Financing of Education.* Gainesville, Florida: National Educational Finance Project, 1970.

BUCHANAN, J. M., and DEVLETOGLOU, N. E. *Academia in Anarchy: An Economic Diagnosis.* New York: Basic Books, 1970.

BUNDY, MCG. "Were Those the Days?" *Daedalus,* 1970, *99*(3), 531–567.

Bureau of Programs and Budget, Executive Office. *Program III. Intellectual Development and Education.* Lansing, Mich.: State of Michigan, Program Budget Evaluation System. August 1971.

Carnegie Commission on Higher Education. *The Capitol and the Campus.* New York: McGraw-Hill, 1971.

Carnegie Commission on Higher Education. *A Chance to Learn—*

An Action Agenda for Equal Opportunity in Higher Education. New York: McGraw-Hill, 1970.

Carnegie Commission on Higher Education. *New Students and New Places.* Hightstown, New Jersey: McGraw-Hill, 1971.

CARTTER, ALLAN M. *An Assessment of Quality in Graduate Education.* Washington, D.C.: American Council on Education, 1966.

CHEIT, E. F. *The New Depression in Higher Education.* For the Carnegie Foundation for the Advancement of Teaching. New York: McGraw-Hill, 1971.

The Chronicle of Higher Education. March 22, 1971, 5(24); May 3, 1971, 5(30), 6; May 10, 1971, 5(31), 2; May 24, 1971, 5(33), 1, 2; November 15, 1971, 6(8), 9; November 29, 1971, 6(10); February 7, 1972, 6(18), 9.

CONWAY, J. "Styles of Academic Culture." In S. R. Graubard and G. A. Ballotti (Eds.), *The Embattled University.* New York: George Braziller, 1970.

CRAEGER, JOHN A. "The American Graduate Student: A Normative Description." *ACE Research Reports,* 1971, 6(5).

CROWL, J. H. "Legislative Issues and Actions Affecting Higher Education in Fifteen States." *The Chronicle of Higher Education.* May 17, 1971, 5(32), 4.

DAVIS, B. H. "AAUP at the Crossroads?" *Change,* 1971, 3(4), 78.

DILL, D. D. *Case Studies in University Governance.* Washington, D.C.: National Association of State Universities and Land-Grant Colleges, 1971.

DRESSEL, P. L. *The Undergraduate Curriculum in Higher Education.* Washington, D.C.: The Center for Applied Research in Education, Inc., 1963.

DRESSEL, P. L., JOHNSON, F. C., and MARCUS, P. M. *The Confidence Crisis.* San Francisco: Jossey-Bass, 1970.

DUNGAN, R. A. "Higher Education: The Effort to Adjust." In S. R. Graubard and G. A. Ballotti (Eds.), *The Embattled University.* New York: George Braziller, 1970.

DURANT, W., and DURANT, A. *The Lessons of History.* New York: Simon and Schuster, 1968.

The Economics and Financing of Higher Education in the United States. A compendium of papers submitted to the Joint Economic Committee, Congress of the United States, Washington, D.C.: U.S. Government Printing Office, 1969.

Education Commission of the States. *Higher Education in the States.* Washington, D.C., 1971.

EPSTEIN, L. D. "State Authority and State Universities." *Daedalus,* 1970, *99*(3), 700–712.

EVANS, J. E., JR. *Collective Bargaining for Technical and Professional Employees.* Chicago: Institute of Labor and Industrial Relations, 1965.

Faculty Participation in Academic Governance. Washington, D.C.: American Association of Higher Education, 1967.

FARMER, J. "Why Planning, Programming, Budgeting Systems for Higher Education?" *Monographs for College and University Presidents,* 1. Boulder: Western Interstate Commission for Higher Education, 1970.

FEINSINGER, N. P., and ROE, E. I. "The University of Wisconsin, Madison Campus—The Dispute of 1969–70: A Case Study." *Wisconsin Law Review,* 1971, *1,* 229–274.

FEINSTEIN, O., et al. *Higher Education in the United States.* Lexington, Mass.: D. C. Heath and Company, 1971.

FINKIN, M. W. "Collective Bargaining and University Government." *American Association of University Professors Bulletin,* 1971, *57*(2), 149–162.

FUCHS, R. F. "Academic Freedom—Its Basic Philosophy, Function, and History." In H. W. Baade (Ed.), *Academic Freedom: The Scholar's Place in Modern Society.* Dobbs Ferry, N.Y.: Oceana Publications, Inc., 1964.

GAFF, J. G., and Associates. *The Cluster College.* San Francisco: Jossey-Bass, 1970.

GIDDENS, P. H. "The 1969 Intercollegiate Football Season in Retrospect." *Liberal Education,* 1970, *56*(4), 532–533.

GLENNY, L. A. *Autonomy of Public Colleges—The Challenge of Coordination.* New York: McGraw-Hill, 1959.

GLENN, L. A., and WEATHERSBY, G. B. (Eds.) *Statewide Planning for Postsecondary Education: Issue and Design.* Boulder, Colorado: National Center for Higher Education, Western Interstate Commission for Higher Education, 1971.

GRAUBARD, S. R., and BALLOTTI, G. (Eds.) *The Embattled University.* New York: George Braziller, 1970.

GROSS, EDWARD. "Universities as Organizations: A Study of Goals." In J. V. Baldridge (Ed.), *Academic Governance.* Berkeley: McCutchan, 1971.

GROSS, E., and GRAMBSCH, P. V. *University Goals and Academic Power.* Washington, D.C.: American Council on Education, 1968.

GULKO, W. W. *Program Classification Structure.* Preliminary Edition for Review. Boulder: Planning and Management Systems Division, Western Interstate Commission for Higher Education, June 1970.

HARTLEY, H. J. *Educational Planning-Programming-Budgeting: A Systems Approach.* Englewood Cliffs, N.J.: Prentice-Hall, 1968.

HEFFERLIN, JB L. *Dynamics of Academic Reform.* San Francisco: Jossey-Bass, 1969.

HODGKINSON, H. L. "A Response to 'Emerging Concepts of the Presidency.'" *The Journal of Higher Education,* 1971, *42*(5), 368–373.

HODGKINSON, H. L. *Institutions in Transition, A Study of Change in Higher Education.* New York: Carnegie Commission on Higher Education, 1970a.

HODGKINSON, H. L. "Presidents and Campus Governance: A Research Profile." *The Educational Record,* 1970b, *51*(2), 159–166.

HODGKINSON, H. L., and MEETH, R. (Eds.) *Power and Authority.* San Francisco: Jossey-Bass, 1971.

HOWE, R. A. "Roles of Faculty." In H. L. Hodgkinson and L. R. Meeth (Eds.), *Power and Authority.* San Francisco: Jossey-Bass, 1971.

IKENBERRY, STANLEY O. *Roles and Structures for Participation in Higher Education Governance: A Rationale.* College Park, Pa.: Center for the Study of Higher Education, The Pennsylvania State University, 1970. Report No. 5.

JACOBSON, R. L. "NLRB Reaffirms Its Jurisdiction in Bargaining at Private Colleges." *The Chronicle of Higher Education,* 1971, *6*(1), 1–3.

JAMES, H. T. "The New Cult of Efficiency and Education." In L. H. Browder, Jr. (Ed.), *Emerging Patterns of Administrative Accountability.* Berkeley: McCutchan, 1971.

JENCKS, C., and RIESMAN, D. *The Academic Revolution.* Garden City, N.Y.: Doubleday & Company, 1968.

KEETON, M., and HILBERRY, C. *Struggle and Promise: A Future for Colleges.* New York: McGraw-Hill, 1969.

KERR, C. "Governance and Functions." In S. R. Graubard and G. A. Ballotti (Eds.), *The Embattled University.* New York: George Braziller, 1970.

KIRK, R. "Massive Subsidies and Academic Freedom." In H. W. Baade (Ed.), *Academic Freedom: The Scholar's Place in Modern Society.* Dobbs Ferry, N.Y.: Oceana Publications, 1964.

KOG, W. T. "Thoughts on Our Future." London: University of Lancaster, February 22, 1971. (Mimeo.)

LAWRENCE, B. "The WICHE Planning and Management Systems Program: Its Nature, Scope, and Limitations." Unpublished Mansucript. Boulder: Western Interstate Commission for Higher Education, 1971.

LIEBERMAN, M. "Professors, Unite!" *Harper's Magazine,* October 1971, pp. 61–70.

LIEBERMAN, M., and MOSKOW, M. H. *Collective Negotiations for Teachers.* Chicago: Rand McNally, 1966.

LIVINGSTON, J. C. "Academic Senate under Fire." In G. Kerry Smith (Ed.), *Agony and Promise.* San Francisco: Jossey-Bass, 1969.

London Daily Telegraph. January 14, 1971; January 20, 1971.

MAYHEW, L. B. *Changing Practices in Education for the Professions.* Atlanta, Georgia: Southern Regional Education Board, 1971.

MAYHEW, L. B. "Emerging Concepts of the Presidency." *The Journal of Higher Education,* 1971, *42*(5), 356–362.

MAYHEW, L. B. "Jottings." *Change,* 1971, *3*(4), 72–74.

MCCONNELL, "FOREWORD." In L. A. Glenny, *Autonomy of Public Colleges—The Challenge of Coordination.* New York: McGraw-Hill, 1959.

MCCONNELL, T. R. "Faculty Interests in Value and Power Conflicts." *AAUP Bulletin,* 1969, *55*(3), 343–352.

MCCONNELL, T. R. "Accountability and Autonomy." Center for Research and Develpoment in Higher Education, University of California, Berkeley. Given at an Invitational Seminar, "Restructuring College and University Organization and Governance," American Association for Higher Education, Airlie House, February 28–March 2, 1971a.

MCCONNELL, T. R. "Faculty Government." In H. L. Hodgkinson and L. R. Meeth (Eds.), *Power and Authority.* San Francisco: Jossey-Bass, 1971b.

MCCONNELL, T. R., and MORTIMER, K. P. *The Faculty in University*

Governance. Berkeley: Center for Research and Development in Higher Education, University of California, 1971.

MCGEE, R. *Academic Janus.* San Francisco: Jossey-Bass, 1971.

MCGRATH, E. J. *The Graduate School and the Decline of Liberal Education.* New York: Institute of Higher Education, Bureau of Publications, Teachers College, Columbia University, 1959.

MCHUGH, W. F. "Collective Bargaining with Professionals in Higher Education." *Wisconsin Law Review,* 1971, *1,* 55–90.

MILLER, F. B. "The Personnel Dilemma: Professor or Not?" *Personnel Journal,* 1959, *38*(2), 53–59.

MOOS, J., and ROURKE, F. E. *The Campus and the State.* Baltimore: Johns Hopkins Press, 1959.

MORISON, R. S. "Some Aspects of Policy-Making in the American University." *Daedalus,* 1970, *99*(3), 609–644.

MORTIMER, K. P., IKENBERRY, S. O., and ANDERSON, G. L. *Governance and Emerging Values in Higher Education.* College Park, Pa.: Center for the Study of Higher Education, The Pennsylvania State University, 1971.

MORTON, B. L. "Perspective from a State Coordinator of Higher Education." *The Educational Record,* 1970, *51* (3) , 296–300.

MOSKOW, M. H. "The Scope of Collective Bargaining in Higher Education." *Wisconsin Law Review,* 1971, *1,* 33–45.

MURPHY, W. P. "Academic Freedom—An Emerging Constitutional Right." In H. W. Baade (Ed.), *Academic Freedom: The Scholar's Place in Modern Society.* Dobbs Ferry, N.Y.: Oceana Publications, 1964.

MUSHKIN, S. J., and POLLAK, W. "Analysis in a PPB Setting." In R. L. Johns, I. J. Goffman, K. Alexander, D. H. Stollar (Eds.), *Economic Factors Affecting the Financing of Education.* Gainesville, Florida: National Educational Finance Project, 1970.

National Center for Health Statistics. *Opening Fall Enrollment in Higher Education, 1970. Institutional Data.* Washington, D.C.: U.S. Department of Health, Education, and Welfare, Office of Education, 1970.

NEWMAN, F., et al. *Report on Higher Education.* Office of Education, U.S. Department of Health, Education, and Welfare, Washington, D.C.: U.S. Government Printing Office, 1971.

NISBET, R. *The Degradation of the Academic Dogma: The University in America, 1945–1970.* New York: Basic Books, 1971.

Ohio Board of Regents. *Program Expenditure Models for Higher Education Budgeting.* Columbus, Ohio: Ohio Board of Regents, 1971.

O'NEIL, R. M. *The Eclipse of Faculty Autonomy.* Berkeley: University of California, Assembly on University Goals and Governance, 1971.

PAKE, G. E. "Whither United States Universities?" *Science,* 1971, *172*(3986), 908–916.

PARKER, GARLAND G. "Statistics of Attendance in American Universities and Colleges, 1970–71." *School and Society,* 1972, *99*(2331), 105–126.

PAYTON, R. L. "Pruning in Academia." Letter in *Science,* 1971, *173*(3992), 103.

PERKIN, H. J. *Innovation in Higher Education: New Universities in the United Kingdom.* Paris: Organisation for Economic Co-operation and Development, 1969.

RITTERBUSH, P. C. "Adaptive Response within the Institutional System of Higher Education and Research." *Daedalus,* 1970, *99*(3), 645–660.

ROOSE, KENNETH D., and ANDERSEN, CHARLES J. *A Rating of Graduate Programs.* Washington, D.C.: American Council on Education, 1970.

ROSENSTEIN, A. B., and CROMWELL, L. "Dynamic Analysis and Design of Engineering Curricula—The Information Base." Los Angeles: University of California, Department of Engineering, 1968.

SANDS, D. C. "The Role of Collective Bargaining at Private Colleges." *Wisconsin Law Review,* 1971, *1*, 150–174.

SCHMIDT, C. *A Guide to Collective Negotiations in Education.* East Lansing, Michigan: Social Science Research Bureau, Michigan State University, 1967.

SCULLY, M. G. "Attacks on Tenure Mount: Limitations Are Proposed in Five States." *The Chronicle of Higher Education,* March 22, 1971, *5*(24), 4.

SCULLY, M. G., and SIEVERT, W. A. "Collective Bargaining Gains Converts among Teachers: Three National Organizations Vie to Represent Faculties." *The Chronicle of Higher Education*, 1971, *5*(31), 1.

SEARLE, JOHN R. *The Campus War: A Sympathetic Look at the University in Agony*. Quoted by Malcolm G. Scully in "A Plea to Give the Faculty More Authority." *The Chronicle of Higher Education*, November 15, 1971, *6*(8), 9.

SHOBEN, E. J., JR. "Cultural Criticism and the American College." *Daedalus*, 1970, *99*(3), 677–678.

SIEVERT, W. A. "Student Association Plans Pilot Project in Unionism." *The Chronicle of Higher Education*, 1971, *6*(1), 3.

SINGLETARY, OTIS A. *American Universities and Colleges*, Tenth ed. Washington, D.C.: American Council on Education, 1968.

Sixth Annual Report of the Vice-Chancellor to the University Court. London: University of Lancaster, 1970.

SLOMAN, A. E. *A University in the Making*. New York: Oxford University Press, 1964.

Southern Regional Education Board. "State Legislation Affecting Higher Education in the South, 1971. Report Number Two: Tennessee, West Virginia, South Carolina, Texas." Atlanta, Ga.: Southern Regional Education Board, 1971. (Mimeo.)

SPAETH, J. L., and GREELYE, A. M. *Recent Alumni and Higher Education*. New York: McGraw-Hill, 1970.

"State College Association's Statement on Academic Freedom." *The Chronicle of Higher Education*, November 15, 1971, *6*(8), 6.

State of Illinois Board of Higher Education. *Master Plan Phase III*. Springfield: State of Illinois Board of Higher Education, 1971.

STEINHART, J. S., and CHERNIACK, S. *The Universities and Environmental Quality—Commitment to Problem Focused Education*. A Report to The President's Environmental Quality Council, Office of Science and Technology, Executive Office of the President. Washington, D.C.: Government Printing Office, 1969.

STICKLER, W. H. (Ed.) *Experimental Colleges, Their Role in Higher Education*. Tallahassee, Florida: Florida State University, 1964.

STRAUS, R. P. "A Younger Economist's Views on the Market." In R. Fels (Ed.), *The American Economic Review*. Papers and Proceedings of the Eighty-Third Annual Meeting of the American Economic Association, December 28–30, 1970.

SUMBERG, A. D. *The Troubled Campus*. Washington, D.C.: American Council on Education, 1970.

TROW, M. "Conceptions of the University: The Case of Berkeley." In C. E. Kruytbosch and S. L. Messinger (Eds.), *The State of the University: Authority and Change*. Beverly Hills, California: Sage Publications, 1970.

TROW, M. "Reflections on the Transition from Mass to Universal Higher Education." In S. R. Graubard and G. A. Ballotti (Eds.), *The Embattled University*. New York: George Braziller, 1970.

University Grants Committee. *University Grants Committee*. London, Her Majesty's Stationery Office, 1970.

University of East Anglia. *Expansion and the School Structure*. Norwich, England: Development Committee, University of East Anglia, 1970.

University of East Anglia. *University of East Anglia 1971–72 Prospectus*. Norwich, England: University of East Anglia.

University of Essex. "A Brief Description of the University of Essex." Wivenhoe Park, Colchester, England: University of Essex, n.d.

University of Essex. *University of Essex 1971–72 Prospectus*. Wivenhoe Park, Colchester, England, n.d.

University of Essex. *Vice-Chancellor's Report, 1969–70*. Wivenhoe Park, Colchester, England: University of Essex.

University of Kent. *Prospectus for Admissions in October 1971*. Canterbury, England: University of Kent.

University of Sussex. *Guide for Applicants 1969–70*. Sussex, England. University of Sussex.

University of Sussex. *The Organisation of the University 1970–71*. Sussex, England: University of Sussex.

VAN DEN HAAG, E. "Academic Freedom in the United States." In H. W. Baade (Ed.), *Academic Freedom: The Scholar's Place in Modern Society*. Dobbs Ferry, N.Y.: Oceana Publications, 1964.

WAYS, M. "Tomorrow's Management: A More Adventurous Life in a Free-Form Corporation." In L. H. Browder, Jr. (Ed.), *Emerging Patterns of Administrative Acountability*. Berkeley: McCutchan, 1971.

WENGER, RONALD H. "Disciplinary Colleges: An Effective Strategy for Reorganizing a Large College of Arts and Science?" University of Delaware, July 1971. (Mimeo.)

Western Interstate Commission for Higher Education. *The Outputs of Higher Education: Their Identification, Measurement, and Evaluation.* Boulder: WICHE, 1970.

WILLIAMS, R. C. "An Academic Alternative to Collective Bargaining." *Phi Delta Kappan,* 1968, *49*(10), 571.

WOLFLE, D. "The Supernatural Department." *Science,* 1971, *173* (3992), 109. By permission of the author and *Science* Magazine.

WOLLETT, D. H. "The Coming Revolution in Public School Management." *Michigan Law Review,* 1969, *67*(5), 1017–1032.

WOLLETT, D. H. "The Status and Trends of Collective Negotiations for Faculty of Higher Education." *Wisconsin Law Review,* 1971, *1,* 18–20.

Index